MEREDITH'S ALLEGORY. THE SHAVING OF SHAGPAT

Published @ 2017 Trieste Publishing Pty Ltd

ISBN 9780649647811

Meredith's Allegory. The Shaving of Shagpat by James McKechnie

Edited by Trieste Publishing Pty Ltd.
Cover @ 2017

www.triestepublishing.com

JAMES MCKECHNIE

MEREDITH'S ALLEGORY. THE SHAVING OF SHAGPAT

Trieste

Meredith's Allegory

THE SHAVING OF
SHAGPAT

INTERPRETED

BY

JAMES McKECHNIE

HODDER AND STOUGHTON
LONDON   MCMX

NOTE.

It is not as seeking to issue this book under the ægis of Meredith's approval that his letter appears here. Such approval as it contains refers not to the present work but to an essay published some years ago on the same subject. Meredith's letter is given because it reveals his opinions not on my work but on his own. It may fail to convince certain folks that "The Shaving of Shagpat" is an Allegory—but it cannot fail to convince them that Meredith at least intended it to be so.

CONTENTS

May 21 _ 1906

Dear Sir,

You have
done as much as could
be done with the abominable
barber. An Allegory is
hateful to the English,
& I gave it clothing to
conceal its frame. But
neither that nor the

signification availed.
Very few even of my
friends have cared to
read this book, & of
those I can count
but two who have
said a word in
favour of it. I regret
to think that although

you may be indemnified
for the cost of publication
your labour will go
unrewarded.

Yours truly

George Meredith

INTRODUCTION

WHY make a riddle of truth, as if truth were not riddle enough in itself? When poser of this sort is put to the defender of allegory, let him know himself in hearing of the triumphant neighings of horse-sense, and maintain respectful silence. Before a tribunal amenable to finer pleadings it may avail him to claim for allegory that it is self-help translated into a literary expedient — that between other books and it the difference is as between giving a man a dinner of venison and showing him the deer-tracks in the forest, inviting him to capture his dinner. For while allegory is provocative and regulative of ideas, it cannot be said to gift them. It is merely an empty mould, stimulating and guiding in us an outflow of thought to its upfilling. To read allegory is thus to read oneself. It is a magnet to draw out

9

and a mirror to reflect a man to himself, so bringing him into possession of the hidden resources of his own thought. For this reason — provided always that the truth concealed be, on its own merits worth finding — must not that game of hide and seek with it, which allegory essentially is, be de-declared of all intellectual games the one whose rewards are noblest?

Among English Allegories "The Pilgrim's Progress" and "The Shaving of Shagpat" form a class by themselves, and stand to each other in remarkable relationship. Never were two works more similar yet dissimilar in all respects. Almost the most popular and almost the least popular work in our language are alike great Allegories — but how different the quality of their greatness! Of Bunyan it must be said that never did great Allegorist play the game of allegory with more merciful moderation. In his hands indeed it was little more than an expedient to enable him to describe man's hidden struggles, his religious experiences, in the form of a story — securing for it the movement, adventure and interest of genuine story. It marks the triumph of his art that he accomplished this object without requiring to put any but the most transparent veil over his truth, that he sustained the illusion while practically using no illusion. It is impossible to analyse art such as his; its secret is the inscrutable secret of simplicity. As a writer Bunyan was supremely great; as an allegorist he was fortunate in his genius, doubly fortunate in its limitations. It is his happy destiny to delight all readers. Even those who consider the framework of his theology somewhat cramped and rigid are constrained to admit that his imagination moves in it with admirable freedom. "The Pilgrim's Progress" though based on theology is independent of its changes. Its destiny, under all changes, is to nestle close to the heart of humanity, because that it itself is so intensely human. Not then as hinting fault, but merely as stating fact, is it said that while to the extent to which he used allegory Bunyan proved himself a great Allegorist, yet the extent was limited. That game at hide and seek with truth which allegory, at its most legitimate, is —

INTRODUCTION

Bunyan played it in most merciful moderation.

It is difficult, on the other hand, to exonerate Meredith from the charge of having played the game fatally well. If guilty, it aggravates his fault that for quite half a century he looked on at men's bewilderment and misconceptions in regard to his work, and yet uttered no word of guidance; that on the contrary — since they could not read his riddle — he seemed not unwilling to have it believed, rather indeed quizzically encouraged the belief that no riddle was intended.

This apparent indifference toward the fate of his great Allegory must surely be traced to something quite other than indifference. Without pretending to know the facts I am prepared to believe that on none of his works did Meredith, to begin with, build such high hopes as on "The Shaving of Shagpat," and that to the keenness with which he felt the shattering of those hopes is due the fact that, though the bent of his genius lay in the direction, he never wrote another allegory. What his experience had convinced him of was not, we may be sure, that he was incompetent to write allegory, but that the public was hopelessly incompetent to appreciate it. There is no indifference so stubborn as that which is rooted in despair, and Meredith's indifference toward the fate of his Allegory was probably of this nature. As to whether the greater grievance lay with him or the public it is difficult to decide. It is true that were the public tastes and capabilities in the matter of allegory raised to the required standard "The Shaving of Shagpat" would be an altogether successful Allegory. It is further true that so far as it can be called a failure, it is so only by reason of its own overloaded greatness, its own too brilliant success. But ought not Meredith to have better proportioned the gift to the receiver? Most writers indeed are themselves so afflicted with mental limitations and indolences that they meet readers on an equal footing — need, if anything, to write up rather than down to them. But with Meredith, nimblest and strongest of mental athletes, it was different. By his lack of consideration for the public he has suffered not only in popularity but, as I think, in some of the elements of true greatness. He who will not defer to others' weakness is apt to trip over his own strength, and — speaking now of his writings generally — evidence of such tripping is abundant. Genius is at its strongest when it turns its strength in upon itself in wise self-suppression. Meredith lacked in that point of strength. His pages are over-loaded with gems of imagination, and though there be no question as to the value of the gems, their crowded mul-tiplicity comes in time to bewilder, even seriously displease. Simplicity, occasional dullness even, would be a relief from the disturbing glories of his style. He would be a greater writer if he were not quite so great. He would give us more if he gave us less. His genius is equal to most things save the task of self-suppression.

Failure in relation to the public though Meredith's Allegory is — when men can take on them to deny that it is Allegory at all, I am put in the pain-ful dilemma of doubting whether it is their candour or their intelligence I

ought to discredit. Perhaps it is a litttle
of both. Not to speak of those many
loopholes in the work which afford un-
mistakeable peeps into an under-world
of meaning — the book everywhere carries a challenge on its face, is indeed,
in its very construction, a challenge.
Fairyland, to be sure, is the land of the
impossible, but even the impossible has
traditional laws and limits. These
Meredith set at nought in such a way
as to show that his visit to that realm
was not made for its own sake, and
in the devout spirit of fictionist. Fairyland was to him merely the way out
to the world of the actual. All along
he had his eye on the actual — hence
his otherwise unaccountable cantrips,
the weight of too complicated and, as
such, inartistic invention ruthlessly dis-
loaded on that ethereal region. "The
Shaving of Shagpat" viewed merely as
a story has many and rare excellences,
but to assert that it is complete in itself,
stands justified by its own open art,
seems to me a manifest misjudgment.
It is a bewilderment, a broken wonder
of a story — too great yet not great
enough to be complete in itself. The

wildness of its fiction makes us suspect that it is meant for more than fiction; its grotesque lawlessness puts us in search of law. Its very construction is thus a challenge. Am I wrong in assuming that readers have quite generally detected this challenge, and that their subsequent denial of it is by way of being a reasoned, I will not say a disingenuous, afterthought? The book seems to have a meaning, but, they argue, if it really had one they would be able to discover it. The fact that they cannot discover it is therefore proof that it has no meaning. It is not so much that men are blind as that they argue themselves into blindness.

In spite of the undeniable difficulties of his work, I claim for Meredith that he is an entirely honest allegorist — one indeed who cunningly conceals the truth, but never by illegitimate devices. The grotesque humour of the book is not the least effective of such devices. Even those who, from acquaintance with his works, know how serious Meredith can be in his mirth, have been taken in by the wild humour of Shagpat. For it is no intellectual jester but

16

the veritable god of laughter they have to do with here, and truly his godship has kept effective guard at the portals of allegory. But neither the humour nor the romance of the book can be counted other than legitimate blinds. For the romance, though possessing a value and beauty of its own, is yet entirely subservient to, made to take its direction from the allegory. Meredith's work is thus practically hidden in nothing but its own light. Its thoughts are its difficulty. Not of course that its thoughts are arcana, or that mastery of them implies knowledge of special philosophy, *ism* of any sort. An allegory whose kernel is an *ism* always permits of easy interpretation. One has but to know the *ism* to possess the key. But the key required for "The Shaving of Shagpat" is nothing less than the knowledge of life itself. Meredith was too wise to affect secret wisdom; too great a thinker to care much for systems of thought. Valuable truth, as he knew, is never secret truth — unless in the sense of being among those open secrets which every wind blows to us and every sight reveals. It is thus the width, the freedom of his thought which constitute its difficulty. Here let it be said that Bunyan and Meredith in their Allegories alike grip life closely, earnestly; dealing not with little truths, but with the greatest, most universal truths known to them. To be sure even in their agreement they differ; but in regard to their main difference too much need not be made. That Christian's struggle is to save his soul while Shibli Bagarag's is to save the world ought not to be considered a point of hopeless antagonism. It is an antagonism which finds practical reconciliation in every worthy life. But while both are sides of truth, much depends on which side receives the emphasis — and here, I think, Meredith was truer to the spirit of Christianity than Bunyan. In fact, though it contains little open reference to Christianity, "The Shaving of Shagpat" is in few if any respects inferior to "The Pilgrim's Progress" as an exponent of the spirit of Christ. Few who have mastered Meredith's work will be likely to question the truth of this statement; to others, I am aware, it must appear absurd.

Bunyan did well to represent his hero as a pilgrim; Meredith did better to represent his as a reformer. Pilgrimage is a term applicable to life in general; but as a noble life is a struggle against evil, it is more closely represented in the character of a reformer — more closely indeed yet with equal catholicity. All right workers, whatever their sphere of work, are to be called reformers. It is the universal occupation of good men. But of course a reformer, in the concrete, is a specialist. It is never the universal he reforms, but always and only the particular: and in directing his energies to that particular he must be called a specialist. But even as specialist he works under universal rules. All reformers, though engaged in dissimilar work, must be similarly equipped with respect to their work. Hence the qualifications necessary for any reformer are the qualifications necessary for all. In point of training also the special is the way out to the universal. Not by toying with many subjects but by wrestling with one, does man acquire a liberal

education. Not to be specialist is to be
dilettante — passport to the realm of the
vague rather than the universal. Shibli
Bagarag, as shaver of Shagpat, was
necessarily a specialist on Shagpatism;
but nowhere is his specialism obtruded.
The Allegory throughout is kept on the
plain of universal truths. It is entirely
catholic.

Bunyan's was an intense imagination.
All it touched it made alive. But it was
not an imagination rich in invention.
His symbolism shows this. It is, for
the most part, a skin-tight symbolism;
concealing the truth in no more serious fashion than a well fitting glove
conceals the hand. Meredith's symbolism, on the other hand, is such as
only the world's greatest master of
metaphors could produce. You never
can exhaust it, seldom can be entirely
sure of it. It is plastic, kaleidoscopic,
catching and reflecting truth at ever
changing angles. If the labour of interpreting Bunyan's symbols is small,
the reward is frequently not great.
What you get is merely the truth, much
as you knew it before, given back
to you. But Meredith's symbols gen-

erally reward your mastery of them
with floods of fresh light. His imagination was of the stuff myths are made
of. In "The Shaving of Shagpat" there
are allegories worthy for invention,
artistic beauty, to rank with the best in
Greek Mythology; while for spirituality,
richness of meaning, they easily sur-
pass the best. Yet Meredith's metaphors
are not to be dealt with over strenuously. Prosaic analysis is what few of
them can bear. They are fairy coin
intended for currency in the mart of
imagination; creatures of the air let me
rather call them — butterflies of thought
— their utmost gift a dip and glint of
wing in the sunshine. To bear in
mind that "The Shaving of Shagpat"
is written with the fine elusiveness of
poetry is to be in the right attitude
for its study.

No gleaning can make bare the field
of allegory. On the contrary, so magical
is the field, that the labours of one
reaper but make possible a richer harvest for those who follow. That is my
justification for attempting this interpretation of "The Shaving of Shagpat."
Far from being certain that I have

succeeded throughout in recovering Meredith's meaning, I may be practically certain that I have occasionally failed. It is well nigh impossible for two minds to see truth at exactly the same angle. But to the extent that what I say is at once true to life and found to fit into the mould of the Allegory, I may claim it to be a correct interpretation. But not correct to the exclusion of other interpretations. Every man reads life in terms of his own experience and idiosyncrasies of thought; and if another can fittingly fill Meredith's moulds with reality other than mine, his interpretation will be as legitimate as mine. But my belief in regard to such other interpretations is that while they may readily supplement and correct, they will not be antagonistic to, or even on their main lines radically different from my own.

THE WOOINGS OF NOORNA

PREPARATION.

NOT as foreseeing but as aspiring to direct the happenings of time do honourable "readers of planets" take on them to predict great things for those of happy birthdower. They predict that they may bring to pass — the right use of prediction. See the case of Shibli Bagarag. Let Shibli Bagarag be true to himself — stand by his tackle — and he will come to great things — said the "readers of planets." Creative prophecy, setting the youth's heart on fire, making him ill at ease amid the delights of Shiraz! Not that he was satiated with these delights — his being still the first keenness of youth; nor that he nourished ascetic scorn of them—a toothsome feast, then as ever, being of honourable consideration and no hog's paradise in his eyes. But to be sitting at ease in Shiraz "partaking of seasoned, sweet dishes,

25

c

dipping his fingers in them" while that prophecy of the "readers of planets" was not fulfilled, nor in smallest way of fulfilment — no longer could he endure the self-scorn of it. It was up and away with Shibli Bagarag, roaming the world, searching it for greatness. Ah, weary search, bitter disillusionment! After he has travelled far, been a tempter of destiny, a picker up of experience in many lands, he comes to us for introduction. At a glance we see things have not gone well with him. On his own confession they have gone deplorably ill. He is hungry, distressed, in need of all things. But greatness — ah, of your charity invite the poor youth to dinner, and taunt him not with wild-goose chase after greatness.

Is not the experience of ambitious youth in general truthfully mirrored here? "Readers of planets," predictors of great things — sanguine parents seldom fail to act as such to their children. But should they fail, children of the right sort are at no loss. Predestination is the creed of humanity, of no portion of it more devoutly so than the youthful. To believe in one's star is to believe

in oneself, and in more than oneself.
Belief in self merely is too narrow a
basis on which to build a noble life.
It is necessary to feel that the universe
is cognisant of you, has place and work
set apart for you, that in the building
of God's temple a certain stone is for
your hands and none other's to place.
If you call this fatalism, call it also,
since it lives only as wedded to action,
by the nobler name of faith. It is the
characteristic of faith that it finds itself
only in action. Action turns the jelly-
fish into the vertebrate, pious dream
into masterful faith. Man never truly
believes until he is at some sacrifice
for belief's sake. Before Abraham could
become "the Father of the Faithful"
he had to turn his back on home and
kindred, grip God by the hand, fare
forth with Him into the unknown. So
with Shibli Bagarag — he who deserted
the "seasoned, sweet dishes of Shiraz,"
faced hunger, misery, peril in search
of great things. Before you can enter
any right path in life you must pay
toll by an act of sacrifice. Always must
there be the giving up of something
in order to seek a better something;

always also the agony of hope deferred in regard to that better something.

Shibli Bagarag's outward condition, at our meeting with him, is bad; but how as to his inward condition? A man, after all, carries his fortune in his heart: if Shibli Bagarag's heart is resolute, the distress of his condition may be merely a sign that he is on the right path, the "steep and thorny road" appointed unto candidates for greatness. On his starting out from Shiraz there was round his soul, screening it from life's realities, a cosy cloak of illusion, woven of self-love and inexperience. What, now that the world has had time to batter it with realities, is Shibli Bagarag doing with this cloak? Is he tearing it from or drawing it desperately round his soul — exposing it to, or patching, thickening it against further batterings of reality? Why as to that — and with Meredith it is the test question of life — you will judge the youth unfavourably if you take serious account of his mouthings, impeachments of the universe in the matter of greatness and dinner, both shamefully overdue. But in the bad old days when

PREPARATION

flogging was the law of the Navy, sailors under the lash had licence of speech, could mouth mutiny and no notice taken. So of your charity deal with Shibli Bagarag, for the words of the desperate are not to be criticised. And note, for it is here that you see the real man, that though the youth laments the loss of the "flesh pots" he makes no motion to return to them, and truly had he been mindful he might have had opportunity to return. The "seasoned, sweet dishes of Shiraz" haunt his imagination, but his will, the citadel of self, remains unmoved. Back to Shiraz he will not go. Say it was only stubbornness, but know that in stubbornness — that last refuge of battered egoism — a man's guardian angel may sometimes shelter. Stubbornness is the will at bay, deserted or seemingly deserted, even by reason, its lawful ally. But reason often visits man incognito: a stubborn man may well be one in receipt of such visit. In Shibli Bagarag's case stubbornness was wisdom.

Is it not time the youth were finding, settling down to work? Consider his ripeness, verging on over-ripeness for

29

work. He has tutored himself into much manhood, has roamed the world, endured—complainingly indeed yet also unflinchingly — hunger, hardship, the worst of fortunes. That golden dream which his ambition was at first setting out from Shiraz—life's disillusionments have not dispelled it, merely hardened it into set resolution. The youth is driven in upon himself to the invigorating, enriching of his manhood. This driving of self in upon self is among the chief gains of life's buffetings. To most candidates for greatness there comes a time — it is their supreme testing time — when their glad, expansive faith in their star seems to condense, shrivel up, become nothing more than a minute, diamond-pointed faith in themselves. They carry then the burden of their destinies in the form of a bare resolution. The stars in their courses fight against them, and they, in divine rebelliousness, fight against the stars in their courses. This is indeed the supreme tonic of the human spirit — this isolation which reveals to it the awful strength of its own spirithood. But to spirit as little as to body

are tonics substitute for food. Shibli
Bagarag for the present has had enough
of tonics; if kept much longer on them
the medicinal bitterness will for him
turn poisonous. His spirit will be de-
voured by its own energies; as an
unused sword it will "eat into itself
for lack of something else to hew and
hack," yea his life being thus a mere
fever will pass altogether out, consumed by its own fires. No further
progress on right lines can Shibli Bagarag make until he finds work. Faults
of character in plenty he still has, but
are they such as in his present position
he can afford to part with? His boast-
ings, for instance, hateful though they
would be in a successful man, are they
not permissible, almost admirable, in
virile failure such as he? Confessedly
he is an inchoate man, his virtues but
crabbed virtues, half-kin to vices, but
what will you have of a failure? 'Tis
the sunshine that sweetens: let Shibli
Bagarag get into the sunshine. Everything he has learned in the school of
failure let him, for his soul's health,
not unlearn but relearn in the school
of success. Then, not till then, may

31

the man be "clothed in humility."

The Unseen Powers have not been disregardful of Shibli Bagarag, nor have they kept him needlessly waiting. His preliminary drill, every hour of it, has been necessary to put him in condition to look at, consent to parley with such messenger as they intend to send. Now that he is in condition Noorna bin Noorka appears, offering him his commission; and 'tis the commission to shave Shagpat.

So broad is Shagpat's back he can bear almost any evil meaning that can be put on him. Every man may therefore in regard to him make "private interpretation." Any established evil, any baneful superstition, any tyranny of lies is Shagpat. To remove an abuse whether in Church, State or village community is to shave Shagpat. All that is demanded is that it be an objective evil, something that hurts the world. Not that the Allegory does not take recognition — it takes very ample recognition — of the existence of, the necessity for shaving inward Shagpats, those Shagpats that abide in and blight the soul of man. None the less it will have no direct tinkering with the soul, for of such tinkering spiritual hypochondria, worse evils come. To secure the blessings of spiritual training without the evils of spiritual tinkering, devotion to the shaving of some Shagpat is necessary. Without such devotion, with its outpouring of healthy activity, man, if he awakens into spirituality at all, can only awaken into morbid spirituality. He becomes a peevish student of symptoms, a feeler of the pulse of his soul; so making hypochondriac havoc of his conscience. For the right development of his manhood it is necessary therefore that he devote himself in loving hatred to the shaving of some one or other of the world's Shagpats. The Allegory is framed in full recognition of this truth. Shibli Bagarag undergoes a strenuous spiritual training, but the direct object of his training is not to save himself, but to make himself a Sword for the saving of men.

As for the Shagpat which Shibli Bagarag is commissioned to shave — if it is for our mental convenience to interpret him with some measure of definiteness,

33

—we may say that he represents a false faith, a faith that dominates, and dominates only to blight, the minds and hearts of men. That would imply that Shagpat is an institution. The law of life is externalisation. Everything is irresistibly driven to create for itself a body: until it has a body it is not strictly among the things that are at all. Shagpat then is an institution, a false faith embodied in an institution. The greatness, wide extent of his power, is a point to be noticed. "There be governments and states, and conditions of men remote, that hang on him, Shagpat." Clearly he stands high in the hierarchy of falsehood, is indeed the reigning falsehood of the day; men for the most part not yet knowing him to be false. Rather do they "crowd and crush and hunger to adore him" being "held in enchantment by him, and made foolish by one hair that's in his head." It is this Shagpat, mighty, enthroned lie — believed in, upheld by peoples and empires — that Shibli Bagarag is commissioned to shave. Truly the youth's opportunity has come at last. Will he have courage to embrace it?

34

HESITATION.

IDEAS prove themselves living by changing, passing into something else, "dying to live." Such an idea is Noorna bin Noorka — creature hence of transformations, surprises. In the story she is represented as conveying to Shibli Bagarag the idea of shaving Shagpat, in reality she is herself that idea personified. It is not however in the abstract, or in relation to men in general, but in relation to Shibli Bagarag that she is so. She is the idea as it strikes, appeals to him, strictly thus *his* idea of shaving Shagpat. As engaging, monopolising his thoughts and activities she of necessity is continually taking on new aspects, breaking out into fresh inspirations, gathering to herself ever richer and more varied meanings. Hence her amazing transformations, necromancies, cantrips. No cantrips would she exhibit were she a

35

still-born idea enthroned — the fate of such — as mummy-idol on the "god-shelf" of the mind; her consistency then would be of the kind to evoke the enthusiasm of fools. But such as she is, Noorna is the heart of the Allegory — the finest and subtlest of allegorical characters.

Were she an academic idea Shibli Bagarag might be writing essays, songs even, in praise of her beauty. But as a practical, imperative idea he finds her repulsive. Many kinds of miracles may happen, but miracles of ugliness never happen. Nevertheless Shibli Bagarag's repugnance demanding, for the intensity of it, such miracle as symbolism, Noorna is depicted as impossibly ugly. Even so he cannot lightly reject her. Repellent though she is to flesh and blood, she yet "instigateth keenly," stirs up, makes such mighty challenge to his manhood that he cannot lightly reject her. Know Noorna therefore for what she is, "Stern Daughter of the Voice of God," member of the Royal Family of the Duties, ugliest marriageable member of the Family! 'Tis a great point in her favour, this ugliness.

HESITATION

Life brings many pleasant duties, their pleasantness making them none the less duties, but through their discharge can no man come to greatness. The duties which bring us our opportunity, through which we discipline our souls, wrestle into strength, glory — all of them are stern, forbidding of feature. 'Tis then a great point in Noorna's favour, her divine ugliness. Here, now that she is of marriageable years, is she, according to the custom of her Family, wooing among the sons of men, seeking some best and bravest youth to be her betrothed. Splendid yet fearsome luck for Shibli Bagarag should he prove the youth. Him will she lead through thwacks into glory!

Meantime 'tis to be taken as no bad sign that he coquettes but squeamishly with Noorna. Men destined to move the world are never of the light-o'-love order, themselves easily moved. They come profoundly rather than rapidly under new influence. The conservative instinct is strong in them, indeed true reformers are almost necessarily conservative at heart. They are too reverent to be cheerfully iconoclastic. The thing that has forced its way into actuality is for them a thing not to be suppressed otherwise than with due hesitation. For they judge that if there is the law of the survival of the fittest, there is also the law of the coming into being of the fittest. The thing that has struggled out of nothingness into being has in their eyes at least a presumptive right to be. Possession is nine points of the law, and existence is nine points of its own justification — so to begin with, the men destined to reform the world often think. Certainly he who enters on the work of reform, especially religious reform, with a light heart is little likely to prove a great reformer. Your very superior cosmopolitan person who can lay his finger inerrantly, in indeed a quite suave omniscience, on the shortcomings and superstitions of human creeds — to be sure it would not cost him a groan to shave Shagpat, and by that token he never can shave Shagpat. To qualify for becoming a liberator of the world a man must generally himself have been in bondage. It is in the process of emancipating himself that he eman-

cipates the world. This accounts for
the gradual nature of Luther's "Reformation," and for the heart-searchings it
occasioned him. He began to be an
iconoclast before he had ceased being
a worshipper, to attack the Church before he had ceased to number himself
among her most dutiful sons. So cherished was his heritage of reverence for
Papal authority that in fighting against
Rome, he felt himself, almost to the
last, fighting against himself. Luther
also had much squeamish coquetting
with his Noorna.

Nevertheless, all allowance being
made, Shibli Bagarag's first concession
to Noorna cannot be described as other
than a too ungallant one. For what
does he, as opening move in campaign,
but make petition to the king — a
monstrously hairy king — saying: "It
is my prayer O King of the age
that thou take me under thy protection, and the shield of thy fair will,
while I perform good work in this city
by operating on the unshorn." Now
questionable in point of expediency and
morals though the policy must appear,
Shibli Bagarag is not necessarily to be

blamed for this attempt to enlist hair
as ally in battle against hairiness. In
great enterprises great risks must be
taken. To be fastidious is to be impotent. To insist that because your
cause is saintly your army must be
composed of saints is to be quixotic.
Had Shibli Bagarag sought this hairy
king's patronage because he believed
it would afford him the best, most
effective means of shaving Shagpat, no
blame might have been his. But that
was not what he was thinking on. How
to save his own skin was what he was
thinking on. This shaving of Shagpat
promises to be dreadful work. It means
nothing less than upsetting the world,
playing havoc with the reverences, the
conservatisms, the superstitions of men;
'tis certain there will be thwacks, stinging ones, going in such an enterprise.
Shibli Bagarag cannot see his way to
undertake it unless his personal safety
is guaranteed. But the king's protection would be a sufficient insurance
policy against thwacks; give him that
and, Allah helping him, he would pro-
ceed to shave Shagpat. Yes, with a
blunted razor, the price, as he must

know, of such a king's protection being
the blunting of his razor. Truly Shibli
Bagarag's first concession to Noorna is
a too ungallant one. It is also, in relation to his own purposes, a foolish
one. The man who aspires to climb
the heights of ambition with an insurance policy against thwacks in his
pocket, is but one of fortune's fools,
with whom good sport will be made.
In a fight downright bravery is the best
coat of arms; and downright cowardice
has at least the negative merit of keeping man out of a fight. But cowardly
courage, in its struggle to face danger
safely, merely exposes itself to the more
abundant danger. None the less since
bravery is not the absence of, but the
triumph over fear, much is to be said
in favour of cowardly courage. Shibli
Bagarag moves indeed in an ungallant
fashion, but please remember he is the
only man gallant enough to move in
any fashion. The important thing, for
the present, is that he is on the move
at all. Heroes are not made in a day;
much thwacking is required for the
making of a hero; and Shibli Bagarag's
luck in this matter is little likely to fail

41

D

him. Fail him it would were the King
to grant his request; a pitiful spectacle
he would then present, hacking feebly
at Shagpat with blunted razor. But
praise the Disposer of Destinies, the
King proves a fool, commands on advice of cunning Vizier Feshnavat that
the youth "be summoned to a sense
of the loathsomeness of his craft by
the agency of fifty stripes." And that
was what came of Shibli Bagarag's in-
genious attempt to take out, at the
expense of Noorna, an insurance policy
against thwacks. The like good fortune
to all who prefer their skin to their
Noorna.

But Shibli Bagarag is not the youth
to abandon his enterprise because he
cannot be guaranteed against danger.
If he does not as yet summon to himself genuine courage, he at least draws
upon the resources of his own san-
guineness, assures himself that after
all the danger is not great. It is not
as if he were Shagpat's enemy, or had
any intention of making war on genuine Shagpatism. The very reverse is
the case. It is because he reverences
Shagpat so, that he hates to see Shag-

pat's disfiguring hairs. His purposes toward the man of hair are genuinely benevolent — as benevolent, say, as, to begin with, were those of Luther towards Rome — why then should he anticipate enmity? "Enter thou to him gaily, as to perform a friendly office, one meriting thanks and gratulation, saying 'I will preserve thee the Identical.'" Thus counselled Noorna, her counsel, here as always, representing the working of Shibli Bagarag's own thought. So modeſt, so manifestly necessary is the measure of reform he contemplates that from no quarter, leaſt of all from Shagpat, need he anticipate serious opposition. Shagpat's hairiness must be a burden to himself. Like as not he is secretly longing for the services of barbercraft, a thing hitherto impossible to be got in this accursed city. When therefore a friendly, conservative shave is offered him, will Shagpat not be glad? Shibli Bagarag will undertake not to remove one hair more than the ſtrict interests of health and decency demand; in any case, and above all, he will undertake that the Magical Hair, the Identical, will not be

43

removed, interfered with in the least degree. Why then should Shagpat not be glad? For this preserving of the Identical means substantial immunity for Shagpat. It means that only certain disfiguring hairs, flagrant abuses, adhering to him are to be attacked, that he in his essential self is to be held sacred, let remain identically as he is. Blame not Shibli Bagarag if in thus limiting the scope of his reform, he has been to some extent influenced by a desire to propitiate Shagpat. Compromise is the law of human relationship. Government means either compromise or tyranny. No reformation accomplished by methods of compromise can indeed be thorough in its nature, but Shibli Bagarag does not, cannot in terms of his present convictions aim at thoroughness. He is a conservative reformer. His ideals are in the past rather than in the future. His aim is not to overturn but to restore, bring back what he conceives to be the good old days of Shagpatian simplicity. His scheme of reform is thus a meagre one, fitted indeed by its meagreness to provoke

44

the scorn of dreamers. But omni-
potence is easy in dreamland. A
dreamer need not limit his dream to
some modest remedying of earth's
injustice; he may as well, when at
it, dream of creating a new heaven and
earth altogether. But for Shibli Bagarag, a practical youth cautiously feeling
his way among things practical, this
modest beginning must be declared
excellent. It gives promise that he
will prove a reformer with progressive
ideals, one working to no stereotyped
plan, but as accepting the guidance of,
likely to guide the march of events.
They who see the shortest distance
before them often go furthest, for as
they aim at no definite goal, no definite
goal can satisfy them. The reform
Shibli Bagarag proposes is confessedly
quite inadequate, but let him set about
it in earnest, taking no further counsel
with the delicacy of his skin, and no
fear but the educative and compulsive
power of circumstances will drive him
far enough.

Note well, as immediate illustration
of the educative and compulsive power
of circumstances, the interview between

the barber and the man of hair. There
is fine condensation of history here;
whole chapters of it, shorn of acciden-
tals yet retaining their full essence, are
here. The reformer and the thing, the
institution, to be reformed — often as
they have stood thus front to front in
friendly, unfriendly conference — when
did ever conference end other than
did this one? Shagpat declines to be
shaved, takes mere mention of shave
as unfriendly act, deserving thwacks.
Things needing to be reformed never
accept, otherwise than on compulsion,
the attention of reformers. Even when
under compulsion they have many devices to wriggle out of such attentions;
one of them, the cleverest, being to
protest that they themselves are reformers. "There's no denying that I need
a shave, but I'll have no barbers about
me. I'm going to shave myself, can
manage it quite well." In that find epitome of not a few historical utterances.
Not however an epitome of Shagpat's
utterance. He being in his might and
not yet knowing fear, delivers himself
of this tit-bit of eloquence:— "A barber!
a barber! Is't so? Can it be? To me?

HESITATION

A barber, O thou, thou reptile! filthy thing! A barber, O dog, a barber? . . . " Howlings, snortings of insensate rage, call you these? Yes, but none the less true representation of the heart thoughts of proud sons of privilege and abuse when reformers would interfere. With their lips they may speak otherwise — lip-masters of polite casuistry they mostly are — but in their hearts it is ever:—"Confound their insolence! How dare they, the unwashed dogs, presume to meddle with us." Verily for the felicity of it Shagpat's speech is a very tit-bit of speech, representative of world-wide Shagpatism. For the rest, and here also in significant irony, Shagpat is an imposing nonentity. To sit in preternaturally vacuous solemnity at his shop-front is the earthly task of Shagpat. What matters it if the head that wears the Magical hair be somewhat brainless? Has he not, as Lord of that Hair, millions of brains at his service? Surely it is enough earthly task for Shagpat that he look preternaturally solemn, and, when in the mood for exercise, loll, twiddle his thumbs a little at shop-front.

Shibli Bagarag's appeal to Shagpat ends in failure, and in the concomitant of failure, thwacks. When the enraged Shagpatians had bestowed on him a very "storm of thwacks" they took him "as he had been a stray bundle or a damaged bale, and hurled him from the city into the wilderness once more."

The youth has tried to take out an insurance policy against thwacks, and failed. Then he has tried to convince himself that there will be no thwacks and discovered his error. What next? For the present there is nothing next. He is benumbed, imprisoned within himself, has no outlooks, hopes or prospects, looks "neither to the right, nor to the left nor above." His brain also has lost activity; the monotony of one thought is in it. "O old woman, O accursed old woman" is his dreary repetition. What help for the sorely bethwacked one? Why, the healings of time. 'Tis a youth of naturally lively wits and sparkling hopes. A little time and he will be looking with eyes keen as ever to the right and to the left and above. But will he ever again look at Shagpat?

DECISION.

MEREDITH is an enthusiast in the matter of thwacks, so much so that in praise of them he forgets to be allegorical, speaks openly, in language to be understood of all. With infinite heartiness, with the reiteration of one who revels in his task, he sings, shouts, preaches the hero-making virtues that lie in "celestial hail of thwacks." The mightiest of tonics is this tonic of thwacks, sure specific for hardening into manhood such as have in them the makings of men. Hence 't is compulsory that all candidates for greatness submit to a Preliminary Examination of Thwacks. That the majority fail, relapse whiningly to their native obscurity is all for good; the chosen few, the men of grit remain, and to them, for their further improvement, the world continues generous in thwacks. Thwacked into greatness,"made perfect

49

through suffering"—it is, in a phrase, the history of consummate men. A barbarous method for the making of heroes, but what will you have? Must not the sculptor chisel the marble to fashion the man? Well for us that the Supreme Sculptor, the "Divinity that shapes our ends" is no sentimentalist.

Whatever other effect Shibli Baga-rag's thwacks may have on him, 'tis certain they have already, and at a leap, greatly advanced his education. He sees deeper into the real nature of Shagpat, knows him now to be no un-willing martyr to hairiness, but one wearing hairiness unabashed, flaunting it in the light of day. Shagpat is cor-rupt at the core; ending not mending ought to be his doom. If Shibli Bag-arag tackles him again, he will bear that in mind. But now that he sees what a thwack-bringing monster this Shag-pat is, will he have courage to tackle him again? Ah, it is just with this question, for him become most import-ant of questions, that the youth is at wrestle in the wilderness. Present with him in the wilderness is Noorna, clothed in her ugliness; and since this

DECISION

is his temptation hour, another also,
not mentioned in the Allegory, is with
him. Noorna's words are:—"I propose
to thee this, and 'tis an excellent pro-
position, that I lead thee to great
things, and make thee glorious, a sitter
in high seats, Master of an Event—
provided thou marry me in sweet marriage." The other, unnamed one's
words are:—"You can't propose to keep
further company with that terror. Twice
already, though you merely coquetted
with her, has she brought the lash upon
your back; judge then what a life she
would lead you were you so mad as
betroth her. Even could she bring you
to greatness, which is questionable,
what would greatness be, purchased at
such a price? In mercy to yourself bid
the thwack-bringing ugliness begone."
Vex not Shibli Bagarag now with gabb-
lings of advice; 'tis his supreme hour,
his temptation in the wilderness, and
in silence only can he gather to himself
his strength. But pray, if you will, he
may know that as matters stand between him and Norna, his soul is
already compromised. Noorna has
wooed him too mightily to accept

rebuff tamely. If leave him she must now, it will not be before she has thrust her claw-fingers into his heart, rifling it of treasure. Pray that Shibli Bagarag may know that.

Decisions which endure into the future have their roots in the past. Not that they come by preordainment, determinism — for surely they are sparks from those unquenchable fires of freedom which burn in the spirit of man. But as for the wood and coals which the sparks set on flame — these if the flame is to endure and prevail, must be the gatherings of a lifetime. Well therefore for the strength of Shibli Bagarag's decision that his whole past enters into it — those creative predictions of the "readers of planets," those starvations, buffetings, hardships endured in many lands. He is a man prepared and disciplined of destiny unto this very hour; hence his decision when he comes by it, is given quietly, almost as mere matter of course. " 'Tis a pact between us, O old woman" quoth Shibli Bagarag to Noorna. The occasion is great enough to justify a vow, but Shibli Bagarag is great enough not

to make one. 'Tis the weak in will
who are mighty in vows; their delusion
being that vows can fortify the will,
turn its weakness into strength. When
man wills effectively his yea is simply
yea, his nay nay. Doubt not now in
any case Shibli Bagarag's earnestness.
He who clings to a cause for which he
has suffered, clings to it in no dilettante
spirit. He is identified with it, cemented
to it by his own blood — for such purposes the best of cements. Shibli
Bagarag is no dilettante, but a man
terribly, dangerously in earnest. Not
as keeping his cowardly courage up by
assuring himself that he will emerge
unscathed from the fight; but as ex-
pecting thwacks, prepared to endure
them, does he this time don his armour.
Real courage — hard, set, open-eyed —
has come to him at last. Quietly
therefore, yet passionately, and in true
sacramental spirit, he devotes himself
to the task of shaving Shagpat, takes
it to him for better or worse, even
as a man takes to himself a bride.
This great, passionate, life-filling choice
it is which is romantically yet accurately represented in the Allegory

53

THE WOOINGS OF NOORNA

by Shibli Bagarag's betrothal to Noorna.

When man makes a good resolution he is apt to judge it an achievement in itself, earning him right to breathing time and self-gratulation. From that spring many dangers; a chief one being that to secure this breathing time he antedates his good resolution, fixes it to come into operation to-morrow. But while to-morrow may take over the good work, it merely passes on the good resolutions of to-day to another to-morrow; so that man thus walks through life a day behind his own purposes, never catching up on them. To-morrow is the battle-cry of fools: let Shibli Bagarag, in this his hour of good resolution, see that it is not his battle-cry. Let him hasten to confirm his resolution by rushing into action — to render his betrothal valid by bestowing on Noorna the "kiss of contract." Any first effort to give practical effect to an unpleasant resolution is this "kiss of contract." Though in the wilderness, if that be taken literally, and out of touch with Shagpat, there are many ways by which he can begin to give practical effect to his resolution to

54

accomplish the shave. He can, for one
thing, begin to set himself in order —
to sacrifice, thrust from him such other
ambitions and loves as are in his heart,
and so make queenly room for Noorna.
Whatever form the "kiss of contract"
may have taken — and it is unnecessary
to be precise in the matter — it was no
relishable love-kiss, merely a sternly
hearty duty-kiss. But such as it was,
behold the effect on Noorna. "It was
as though she had been illuminated, as
when a light is put into the hollow of
a pumpkin." Every change in Noorna
symbolises, as has been seen, a change
in Shibli Bagarag himself. The change
here symbolised is that which invariably comes from brave discharge of
unpleasant duty. The unpleasantness
in part disappears; rather not at once
disappears, but — Meredith's symbolism
being entirely accurate — is lit up with
wondrous promise of disappearance.
It is the crosses man refuses to carry
which weigh most heavily on him. He
cannot long hate the duty he honestly
tries to do; there is hidden divinity in
duty to render that impossible. Shibli
Bagarag is already in the way of

making this glad discovery, and it comes to him as reward for running in advance of himself, nobly violating his feelings by kissing Noorna before he loves her. It is continually necessary that a man should in this sense be false to his feelings if he would be true to himself. In temporary divorce between action and feeling — action running nobly, aspiringly in advance—lies man's possibility of progress. Shibli Bagarag is indeed in the way of making glad discoveries. He has kissed the cross, and already there shines through it the lustre of the crown. He has taken upon himself an unpleasant duty, and already his is the promise of glory and of joy.

The temptation in the wilderness is over, and the youth — now worthy to be called the reformer — comes forth victorious. Count it not against him that for the present there is little saint-ship in his victory. If a man delays doing good till his motives are alto-gether good, his delay will be eternal. God does not despise the sacrifice of mixed motives, provided there is some element of good in the mixture. Shibli Bagarag is driven to shave Shagpat by

56

revenge, ambition, any worldly motive you like; but he is also driven to it by the sense of duty. Let him keep that sense of duty, and all will come well. Duty is of the nature that it cannot abide to be one among a democracy of motives. It is the young cuckoo in the nest of the heart; no rest can it take till it expels the other nestlings. Shibli Bagarag is inspired by many motives now; let him keep the motive of duty, and in time he will be inspired by it alone.

Meantime he comes forth from his temptation that rarest, terriblest of beings — an entirely resolute man, single-pointed of purpose, prepared to wait, to work, to suffer. The supreme secret of success is his, revealed to him in that lonely wrestle in the wilderness. It is in solitude, under the private tuition of God that life's best lessons are learned. Even the art of masterful publicity comes by the schoolings of solitude. Take account then of him who comes from the wilderness into the city; the power of God may be upon him to shake the city. It is as a friendless, resourceless youth Shibli Bagarag re-

E

turns to the city of Shagpat; but what of that? He brings with him a magical magnet, found by him in the wilderness and named the magnet of earnestness: doubt not that friends and resources will soon be his. Already one man, attracted by the magnet, is seeking friendship. It is Vizier Feshnavat. The crafty Vizier while outwardly the most zealous, barber-thwacking of Shagpatians, is Shagpat's secret enemy. His heart's desire is to have that miracle of hairiness abased, shaved even to the Identical. But to set bravely about the shave himself is beyond Feshnavat. At best he is merely a go-between, unfit to betroth Noorna but doing his best to seek out, urge some other man to betroth her. He has taken note of Shibli Bagarag as he stood before the King, has heard of his subsequent daring interview with Shagpat; and by these tokens knows that this is the man of men for his purpose. It is fated that the Vizier and the Barber shall meet, for

> "Chance is a poor knave;
> Its own sad slave;
> Two meet that were to meet:
> Life's no cheat."

DECISION

Despise not Feshnavat, the go-between; rather imitate him. If you cannot yourself betroth Noorna, help her to betrothal; the duties you thus do by proxy are well pleasing unto God. Borrowing is the supreme royal art; all rulers of men are great borrowers. If you lack strength to accomplish your desire, borrow another man's strength, even as Feshnavat borrowed the strength of Shibli Bagarag. The next best thing to possessing great qualities yourself is to be able to detect and utilise the great qualities of others.

In other respects Feshnavat is not a man to be admired. He is a trader in treacheries, holds his viziership in virtue of treachery; cannot, it would seem, do even honest work otherwise than in a roguish manner. Ought Shibli Bagarag to accept alliance with such a man? Not to speak of the risk of it, would it be right? Why, if Shibli Bagarag is going to shy at risks, dabble in casuistical scruples, Noorna has made a poor bargain in her betrothal. In loyalty to her he is bound to accept Feshnavat's alliance; not to be sure handing himself unreservedly over to

be a cat's paw in the hands of that wily
one, but retaining watchful independence even in alliance. This is what
happens. By written agreement, properly attested, Shibli Bagarag binds
himself anew to the great task, gives
Feshnavat pledges of loyalty. That is
what is meant by the ceremony of
betrothal, carried out with all due
formalities, in the palace of the
Vizier.

The second kiss, given by Shibli
Bagarag at this ceremony, need be
noticed only for its effect on Noorna.
"New light seemed in her: and it was
as if a splendid jewel was struggling
to cast its beams through the sides of
a crystal vase smeared with dust, and
old dirt, and the spinnings of the
damp spider." What a little thing
enables the gods to work miracles!
Shibli Bagarag solemnly binds himself
to be loyal to his ugly Noorna, and
behold from the core of her ugliness
there already come rewarding radiances,
breakings out of bliss, flashings and
promisings of a beauty that is to be.
Every ugly duty can be kissed into
beauty. Repellent Noornas are of the

blood-royal of Heaven: Heaven awaits those who betroth them.

The moral effect of this alliance on Shibli Bagarag is cunningly symbolised in the Allegory. We can seldom be altogether sure of our beliefs until we see them shared in by others. Thought may take origin in solitude but it gains strength, self-assurance only in society. We need to make converts before we quite realise our own conversion. It means much therefore to Shibli Baga-rag that, at this stage, his idea of shaving Shagpat should be shared in by anyone. The fact that it is shared in, has indeed been first thought of by so great a man as the Vizier — is not Noorna his daughter? — gives the idea added dignity, importance — social stat-us, say — in the eyes of the youth. This change in the attitude of Shibli Bag-arag toward the shaving of Shagpat is expressed, here as always, by a corre-sponding change in Noorna; this time, and note the appropriateness of it, by a change, a queenly magnificence of raiment. Suitable as romance and sig-nificant as allegory is it that Noorna should appear for betrothal "sumptuously arrayed, in perfect queenliness, her head bound in a circlet of gems and gold, her figure lustrous with a full robe of flowing crimson silk. . . . " The reference here, be it said, is to a class of allegorical minutiæ which will not in this exposition receive much attention. The student ought however to be on the outlook for them himself. They abound everywhere, and in them much of the convincingness and beauty of the Allegory resides.

Noorna, member of the Royal Family of the Duties, ugliest marriageable member of the Family, has been wooing among the sons of men, seeking some best and bravest youth to be her betrothed. She has succeeded, and surely there is joy in Heaven over her success. Shibli Bagarag, youth prepared and disciplined of destiny, has accepted the terrible honour of her betrothal, let himself forsooth be thwacked into it. But what then? Others let themselves be thwacked out of it; count it wholly to his honour that he has let himself be thwacked into it. They are betrothed indeed who are wooed into betrothal by thwacks,

DECISION

and Noorna may count on their loyalty. Verily Shibli Bagarag promises to take high rank among the aristocracy of servants, which is the ancient aristocracy of the Kingdom of God.

THE QUEST OF THE SPELLS

INSIGHT.

NO use measuring the oil in the Widow's cruse unless you can also measure the oil that may come into it. It is a miraculous cruse, in touch with, tapping all the resources of oil there are. The measure of the widow's need of and receptacles to store the oil — that is the measure of the oil. So with man's powers. They are determined by his needs and receptivities, in other respects quite indeterminate. By that explain Noorna's magic. She constitutes for Shibli Bagarag a great need and stirs him to a large receptivity. She is his ambition — now that she is betrothed that is her lawful name — and all the genuine magic, the natural magic of human achievement comes through those qualities of earnestness and faith which are the constituents of right ambition. Earnestness multiplies a man, makes him a tenfold, hundred-

fold man: faith puts him in condition
to tap the resources of the Infinite. The
case then with Shibli Bagarag simply
is that being fired and elevated by ambition, he develops in himself the
amazing resources which are attributed
to the magic of Noorna. Great tasks
draw forth great powers, and the help
which Noorna gives the youth is simply
that the youth himself is made larger
and wiser by the fact that he has now
a definite and commanding aim in life.
Not till a man gets such an aim does he
get grip of his own greatness. The "I"
which is "yet not I" puts divine magic,
treasures of insight and strength, at the
service of men who live strenuously.
Every rightly ambitious man is greater
than he knows. He has his spirit-bride,
Noorna bin Noorka, the "sorceress en-
sorcelled" by whom wonders come.

All right success is heralded by, made
possible through failure. Fools may
fail and get no benefit by failure, but
Shibli Bagarag has stored the treasures of failure in his heart. He knows
now that with his present tackle — ac-
complishments — he can never hope to
shave Shagpat, that only one sword,

the sword of Aklis is equal to that.
With aspiring humility and cautious
daring he sets out in quest of those
spells which are the price of this sword.
He has need of his caution. By his
tentative efforts at a shave he has
brought notice on himself, put the
Shagpatians on their guard. His weakness so far has proved his security, but
if caught meddling with Shagpat again,
something more than contemptuous
thwacks may be his portion. Shibli
Bagarag does well therefore to make
the first move in his campaign the turning of Karaz into an "enchanted ass."
Karaz is the chief champion, the effective defender of Shagpat. If given his
widest signification he may be called
the Antagonist, the Evil Principle,
world-wide originator and supporter
of abuses. But the Allegory merely
demands that we view him as the
defender of the Shagpatian abuse, at-
taching to him as such the widest, freest
of meanings. To turn Karaz into an
enchanted ass, type of all stupidity,
what is it but to befool the enemy,
put him off his guard? "Whom the
gods wish to ruin they first make mad"

69

or stupid, an uninteresting but equally effective form of madness. No strength can compensate for stupidity; the more you arm a stupid man the more you hasten his downfall. Simple is the necromancy which Shibli Bagarag practises on Karaz. A victory easily gained is apt of itself to make an enchanted ass of the victor. All Shibli Bagarag has to do is to lie low, let it be believed that he is done for, thwacked into cowardly quiescence, and the vainglorious Shagpat affects to take his triumph sleepily. Pity 'tis that hairiness should breed barbers, but Allah for the unsettlement of men hath decreed it so. The meddlesome rogues, the crackbrained disturbers of things, 'tis certain they can't see a hair without itching to shave it. But Shagpat has thwacks for them, wallahy! he will thwack them one and all until they howl. Meantime a good day's work has been done. Shibli Bagarag, barber, has got his quietus, been thwacked to such purpose that he'll never want to handle razor more. Is it not a good day's work? Shagpat by your leave will go to sleep. That belike was how the enchantment worked,

70

though those who care to study Noorna's necromantic mummery will be rewarded by glimpses of further meaning.

But an ass is a serviceable creature; 't were pity if Karaz were to be let spend his brief asinine days unprofitably. You do wrong if you do n't turn your enemy's folly against himself. His stupidity is your legitimate weapon. Make it minister to his defeat, perhaps so you may teach him certain lessons which will go far to compensate him for defeat. Shibli Bagarag has need of Karaz at any rate. None but Karaz can help him toward certain of those spells which are the price of the Sword. While the enchantment holds then let him mount and away.

These are the Spells which Shibli Bagarag acquired:

The first was a phial of water from the Well of Paravid. Virtue was in that water to make inanimate things vocal, to cause all creatures to speak truly the thing that was in them. What can this be but insight, "the seeing eye and the understanding heart"? The power to get at facts, to see through

men and matters, ranks first among the
Spells. Better insight and nothing else,
than all other things without insight.
A blind Samson, even when benevolent,
is ever a danger. Though he may mean
to hold up the house there is risk that
he will pull it down. The man of
action, who is merely a thinker writing
his thoughts not in books but in deeds,
requires above all things the Water of
Paravid. Napoleon, the world's greatest man of action, had it, carried it
with him into his battlefields; by it
he made the hills and woods to speak,
instructing him to conquer. Be it understood that this Water of Paravid
signifies not so much the power to
collect as the power to estimate facts.
A man may be an industrious collector
of facts, and yet fail to master their
significance. The virtue of the Water
is that it makes facts *speak*, reveal their
true value and significance. It is this
which constitutes it a mighty spell.

This spell never comes unpurchased,
by pure grace of nature. To get it one
must cross a weary desert, which is
the desert of study. Well surely is it
called a desert, for though truth is

refreshing as water, the search for it brings much weariness, thirstiness of doubt. A paradox and yet a statement of law it is that you must go to the desert in search of the waters, that every "land flowing with milk and honey" is reached by way of the wilderness. But note in regard to Shibli Bagarag that 't was on the back of Karaz he passed the desert, and that he lingered not but scurried through it with all possible dispatch. Therein he is an example. Venture not into that doleful desert on foot, nor even on some slow-ambling philosophic nag, else will you leave your bones to bleach there. Go with some definite object, mounted on some Karaz, and see that Karaz lingers not by the way.

It was not as a searcher after truth in general that Shibli Bagarag sought the well. The truth in regard to Shagpat was what he was after. His object was to get at the facts of the case, to master the problem of Shagpatism. Hence Karaz, as champion of the Shagpatian delusion, could alone carry him to the well. Whether in the form of enchanted ass or fire-breathing genie,

F

there was no help for it but Shibli
Bagarag muſt mount Karaz. It is only
from the facts you can learn the facts,
and close personal touch with them is
necessary. If the back of Karaz is too
dangerous or too filthy for your
mount, let that be the end. There is
no going to the well by proxy, giving
commission to another to mount and
bring you the water. Nor is it permitted you before you mount Karaz
to put great coverings on his back to
keep you from touch of his repulsive-
ness. If you are faſtidious with respect
to filth you will never do much to
cleanse the world.

As a rule it is not difficult to keep
Karaz in the form of an enchanted ass
while he carries you to the well. Even
though he perceives you are in search
of truth, yet will the enchantment
generally hold. For the world's great
lies seldom quite know themselves to
be lies. The fact that they have place
among the things that are, that they
are rooted in the established order of
society, gives them a blinding sense of
reality, security. Shagpat does not see
why he need fear inveſtigation. Let

Shibli Bagarag by all means investigate, if such be his humour. What harm can the inquisitive youth do Shagpat? Shagpat will yet know better. The only thing fatal to a lie is truth. It cannot be crushed by persecution — Satan being able to flourish under martyrdom as well as his betters — but at touch of the water of truth it shrivels up into primitive nothingness. But darkness is arrogant in blunders. The thing to be reformed always, though unwittingly, helps the reformer to the truth by which he reforms it. Papacy actively helped Luther to his insight into the errors of Papacy. Like an enchanted ass, type of all stupidity, Rome sent her creatures to hawk indulgences through Germany, thereby compelling Luther to open his eyes, carrying him at breakneck speed to the water of Paravid. It is always so in life. Men see the right by the assistance of the wrong. They are carried to truth on the back of falsehood. Error plays the ass and helps the reformer.

The description of the Well is finely significant, and entirely catholic in every detail. Round it sat idlers,

75

bubble-blowers, players with the waters. These are dilettante students, strenuous triflers, industrious dabblers in intellectual pursuits; and of them great portion of educated society is composed. They play with truth for the refined amusement it affords them, but never plunge boldly into the Well, to emerge therefrom with bleeding hand, carrying treasure. Truth in its saving power is not for those who seek it out of curiosity. Aimless livers cannot be clear thinkers. The waters of Paravid are for those only who have betrothed their Noorna. It is not a little knowledge that is a dangerous thing. It is when men play with knowledge, acquire and hold it without moral earnestness, that there is danger; and then indeed the greater the knowledge the greater the danger. The intellectual without the spiritual, knowledge without earnestness is a peril to the soul. Either do n't meddle with truth at all, or else plunge boldly into the well.

A miracle and no less is this Well of Paravid. "The sky is clear in it, cool in it, and the whole earth imaged therein." So suggestive, so grandly free is the symbolism, it would be sin to cramp it into definite meaning. But take it, if you like, to represent the heart of man — that implies no cramping. Were the water of the heart unfouled by vice, unruffled by passion, the things of heaven and earth would be reflected therein. Nothing images all things but man who is himself all things.

The Well seemed "of the very depth of the earth itself," yet Shibli Bagarag's report of it was: "No sooner had I touched the bottom of the Well than my head emerged from the surface." Is it not always so in the quest after truth? You may dive deep, lose yourself for a time in the waters of doubt and difficulty, yet the moment you solve the problem — get to the bottom of the Well — all is clear, you are in daylight immediately. Simplicity is the hall-mark of truth. The proof that you really understand a thing is that you detect its simplicity. The proof that you have reached the bottom of the Well is that you behold the daylight.

Shibli Bagarag has secured a phial of the water of Paravid. Though the phial is labelled "Shagpatism," let it not be thought that its virtues are limited to giving him knowledge of and insight into that special problem. The special is the way out to the universal. By mastering one subject, especially such a great social subject as Shagpatism, Shibli Bagarag has developed himself generally, widened his mental outlook, become more capable of grappling with, piercing into the truth of all things. The phial would be serviceable to him for any purpose, but none the less it is binding on him to devote it specially to one. It is not for him to wander excursively over the fields of life, dabbling in many interests. As betrothed his liberty is curtailed. Under the auspices of Noorna the phial has been secured; in the services of Noorna it must be spent.

ENTHUSIASM.

T HE next spell to be acquired was three hairs from the tail of the horse Garraveen. It was the horse "heroes of bliss bestride on great days." "Speed quivered on his flanks like lightning." To mount him was to feel oneself on a "bounding wave of bliss." Manifestly this glorious creature symbolises enthusiasm. Its fire and freedom, "dark flushes of ireful vigour," finely suggest the inspired ease, the fierce delight of an enthusiast in his work. Enthusiasm, equally with insight, is necessary for high achievement. It is the God-intoxication of the soul, the mood and the moment of genius; great things are done in it. Enthusiasm without knowledge makes a man a firebrand, dangerous to the state; knowledge without enthusiasm makes him not indeed negligible — the man who *knows* is never negligible — but one who in his own person can accomplish but little.

The horse was made to come by Shibli Bagarag blowing the Call of Battle; it was caught by being struck on the fetlock by a Musk-ball; it was tamed by having the figure of the Crescent traced between its eyes. These three actions represent three forms of enthusiasm — the three hairs which make the spell. The horse coming at the Call of Battle symbolises the warrior's joy, the "stern delight of battle with one's peers." Such enthusiasm is an affair of the blood, a mere pugilistic fervour; but in respect of its strength-giving qualities — and that is the point of the Allegory — it takes worthy rank among the three hairs. Opposition — the Call of Battle — sooner than anything else puts a man on his mettle. Luther confessed that he never was at his best until roused, made angry by opposition. All great men of action in that matter resemble Luther. The joy of battle is their strength.

This enthusiasm may be partly acquired, but it comes mainly by the grace of nature. No man can be a soldier without drill, but drill itself never made a soldier. Shibli Bagarag has always had this war-instinct. There is battle in his blood. Shagpat thinks he has given him his quietus, thwacked him into quiescence. He will yet know that these thwacks were but the Call of Battle, putting Shibli Bagarag on his mettle, bringing him Garraveen, the mighty horse.

The Musk-ball may be said to signify sensuous glamour, and in connection with the horse Garraveen to indicate the enthusiasm which comes from genuine delight in work. It is the joy of the artist in his high creative flights, the glad, passionate activity in which irksome elements of drudgery vanish and purposes are accomplished with happy ease. This form of enthusiasm is at once the inspirer and rewarder of the world's best work. Genius is extasy, brings in its workings the joy of extasy. It is the "I" merged and sublimated in the "yet not I," man carried out of and so entering into kingly possession of himself. Genius may have as its concomitant the "faculty of taking infinite pains," but in

itself genius knows nothing of pains.
It is an inspired state; could it continue, be Shibli Bagarag's in dependable
possession, he would scarcely need
other strength. But of necessity it can
be his only in brief and fickle visitation.
There are ploddings, drudgeries, drab
and dreary toils before him, and for
these he needs another strength. The
Call of Battle enthusiasm, the Musk-
ball enthusiasm for his great moods,
his stirring, dramatic moments; but
that he may be loyal on his dismal
days, cope with life's routine of uninteresting duties, Shibli Bagarag must
have a *lame* Garraveen — a drudge's
enthusiasm. Though enthusiasm, by its
nature, is that which banishes drudgery,
yet the phrase, drudge's enthusiasm,
implies no contradiction. For enthusiasm banishes drudgery by the paradox-
ical method of teaching man mightily
to drudge. God's way is to lead man
out of the wood by driving him further
into it, to bring him salvation from
drudgery by making him an enthusiastic
drudge. A drudge's enthusiasm is dis-
tinguished from, ennobled above other
enthusiasms, in that it is purely an

ENTHUSIASM

affair of the will. There are periods
when all that is good in a man must
retire into his will, find there its sole
conscious existence. Love is normally
a sentiment, an emotion, rather than
a direct affair of the will. Yet there are
moments — they are its tonic moments
— when love's glad expansiveness, its
rainbow-tinted emotions quite vanish,
when it consciously exists not as sentiment but as pure volition. The verb
to love has an imperative mood, and
it is in such mood it confirms, reinvig-
orates itself, finds its nobility. So is
it with a drudge's enthusiasm. It is
enthusiasm of the bare will, enthusiasm
divorced from its extatic delights,
its easy and spontaneous strengths,
stripped indeed of all its sweets, made
an affair of mere tenacity, stubbornness
of purpose. No God-intoxication of the
soul does this sort of enthusiasm seem,
rather, maybe, a God-desertion; but
man is never so near God as when he
serves Him uncheered by the light of
His countenance. For verily there is
divinity in drudgery. God tingles in the
warrior's nerves, flashes in the artist's
brain, hides incalculable in Godhood

83

in the drudge's heart. In drudgery
lies the root enthusiasm of life. Every
drudge is in training to be a genius.
If the world's best work is never
drudgery, yet without drudgery the
world would have no best work.
Wanted then this mightiest among
spells, a drudge's enthusiasm. Wanted
Garraveen, the glorious horse, to be
tamed, yoked, set to the plough. Garraveen, let it be admitted, can be tamed
by many means. Satan has his drudges
as well as God, nor are they behind
God's in enthusiasm. Men oftimes
prove their divinity by the thoroughness with which they violate it, the
mightiness of their drudgery to attain
paltry and unworthy ends. Garraveen
can indeed be tamed in many ways,
but for arduous, world-helping work
such as Shibli Bagarag is engaged in
one power alone can permanently suf-
fice. It is religion — tracing the sacred
sign of the Crescent on the forehead
of the horse. But why religion? Could
not the sense of duty serve Shibli
Bagarag as well? Maybe, but as matter
of fact the world's great exemplars of
duty have, perhaps without exception,

been devoutly religious men. For
somehow the sense of duty, when it is
strong enough to urge to great self-
denials, seems inevitably and in the
nature of things to find for itself religious sanction. Duty is so near God
that the man who grasps duty grasps
God also. It is vain therefore to exalt
duty to a position of independence;
duty itself repudiates independence,
clings for sanction to the throne of
God. Rationalism cannot explain why
this should be so. Man is too deep
for his own fathoming. He cannot
solve the mystery of his own spirit,
make clear to himself the secret that
underlies its instincts and impulses.
Anyhow 'tis certain that the Allegory
here grips the truth of things. Shibli
Bagarag knows Noorna as duty; if he
would be altogether loyal to her his
heart must further acknowledge her to
be divine, know her to be indeed "Stern
Daughter of the Voice of God." Nothing can enable him to drudge enthu-
siastically at the world-helping work he
has undertaken but religion — the sacred
sign of the Crescent on the horse's
forehead. To be altogether strong, to

85

be broad based in his strength, to
have that calm, continuous enthusiasm
which, as nearly as may be, is independent of the tides of blood, the
moods and fluctuations of spirit, it is
necessary that Shibli Bagarag should
know himself in that humblest yet
noblest of capacities — servant of God,
mouthpiece of the Universal. He who
seeks his own glory sickens at even
while he pursues the search: he who
seeks God's glory grows in ardour with
the years. The horse Garraveen is
lamed, made capable of drudgery by the
power of religion. This spell, third and
mightiest in that trinity of strengths
which are the three hairs, will outlast
the others, be at every time available.
The time may come when, sobered
and unmettled by age, Shibli Bagarag
will no longer be as a war-horse neigh-
ing at the Call of Battle. The time may
come when, broken and weary, the
Musk-ball will quite fail of its glamour,
and work be mere drudgery. Even so
he will not faint nor grow weary. The
mark of the Crescent, the seal of God,
is on his spirit. "As sorrowing yet al-
way rejoicing" he can endure to the end.

86

ENTHUSIASM

Youthful enthusiasm cannot be altogether circumspect; it would argue lack of enthusiasm if it were. The art of combining zeal with discretion comes only with the years, with time's educative burden of blunders. But blunders are educative in no other sense than that they have to be paid for; and while God keeps the avenging of crimes in his own hands, he entrusts to fortune the task of avenging blunders. Shibli Bagarag blunders and suffers. He refuses to dismount from Garraveen, that "bounding wave of bliss," laughs at Noorna's warnings about the "red pit of destruction." Woe to the rider when Garraveen gets the bit between his teeth. Enthusiasm must be held in check, made subject to the manifold restraints of patience and policy. Perhaps never yet came the right by quixotic and untimely tilting against the wrong; only such poor judges are we of the times and seasons that we can seldom positively tell when tilting is untimely. Shibli Bagarag's fault was not that he erred in judgment, but that he altogether neglected to judge. He simply let his zeal run away with him. Under discreet treatment Karaz might, some little time longer, have remained an enchanted ass, subservient to uses. But the unveiled and intemperate policy of the reformer broke the spell. Karaz became resentfully awake, no longer an ass but a mighty genie, and at his hands Shibli Bagarag suffered a most sobering fall.

IDEALISM

THE third Spell to be acquired was the Lily of the Enchanted Sea. It was a Lily of surpassing beauty and, for such was its virtue, it was the ordeal of beauty for all things. Nothing earthly, not the fairest of human characters, not the best of human institutions, but blinked and grew blemish-marked in its presence. What can this terrible Lily be but the Ideal, the soul's vision of what ought to be? That is the dream which puts to blush earth's best reality. And since it is on its aesthetic side that a man's Ideal appeals to him, since the good visions itself as the beautiful, could anything more fitly symbolise it than the Lily in its sweet and stainless beauty?

Without this Lily Shibli Bagarag would have been no reformer, but a blind and bungling iconoclast. The

89

reformer must have the prophetic vision, must see the things that are not if he would helpfully meddle with the things that are. Yet he must not be an uncurbed dreamer picturing expansively to himself a new heaven and a new earth unrelated to, not to be evolved out of, the old. The reformer's dreams must be practical. Be his head however high in the clouds, his feet must keep level with earth. It was happily so with Shibli Bagarag. In his search for the Ideal he took constant counsel with the actual. The Water of Paravid — insight into things as they are — was had recourse to on every occasion of doubt. To understand the actual is to perceive the ideal. Never in the realm of unchecked dreams, but only in the actual, bound up with it, emerging out of it is the true ideal to be found. Hence it was that Shibli Bagarag, the practical reformer, continually used the Water of Paravid to guide him to the Lily of the Enchanted Sea.

Put it that Karaz were still an enchanted ass, could his back have served Shibli Bagarag on this as on former

quests? It seems impossible. Shibli
Bagarag in this quest had to be as a
free spirit "voyaging through strange
seas of thought alone." Not the back
of Karaz, but a finer conveyance, even
the cockle-shell of imagination, could
serve him now. None the less 't was
a misfortune — the untimely disenchant-
ment of Karaz, for were he still in his
asshood, though he could not help, he
would not hinder. He would eat the
thistles of idleness, no menace to Shibli
Bagarag. As it is, Karaz, malevolent
genie, has now to be reckoned with.
His first effort, a cunning one, is to lead
Shibli Bagarag astray by an appeal to
the youth's easily roused vanity. At
the flatteries of Karaz, disguised as a
sea-captain, Shibli Bagarag "puffed his
chest, and straightened his legs like a
cock, and was as a man on whom the
Sultan had bestowed a dress of honour." If he can be kept in this humor,
hopeless must be his quest after the
Lily. A man may be vain and yet a
true thinker, but to the extent that he
puts his vanity into his thinking his
thought is vitiated. Thinking is an impersonal process; cannot bear the taint

of selfhood. Especially true is this of Shibli Bagarag's present thinking. Ideals of whatever kind adumbrate God, bring man fearsomely near to God. It must be in the spirit of worship man struggles after the ideal. Shibli Bagarag by struggling after it in the spirit of vanity has put himself out of the way. His going on board ship with Karaz is merely the symbol of this spiritual errancy. Alas that Noorna is not by his side now, surely her counsels are necessary and by them alone can he hope to prevail. The story has it that Noorna had to take leave of her betrothed in order to "counteract the machinations of Karaz." But her betrothed being the butt of these machinations, suffering this moment under them, is it not by his side and nowhere else that Noorna, as counter-actor, ought to be? But in this matter the wording of the story fails to convey the subtle truth of the Allegory. The fact is that Shibli Bagarag, in his quest of the Ideal, could not carry with him as conscious ambition, ever present sense of duty, the idea of shaving Shagpat. The quest even of practical ideals carries a man, in some sense, away from the practical. He must seek the Ideal for its own sake, and with no ulterior object in view. To the extent that he has ulterior object, however worthy, in view, he must be said to fail in pure loyalty to the Ideal. The truth has its uses; but if it is sought primarily for its uses it is not worthily sought, and will scarcely be rightly found. It is well then for Shibli Bagarag that he is not accompanied by Noorna in his quest of the Lily. But note that while his ambition is in abeyance, it is only consciously so. It has ceased to be the thing thought on, but it has not ceased, cannot cease, to be the power behind his thought. So closely has it gripped him that he does not need to be thinking on it to be under its influence. It has passed into his subconscious self, that subliminal region, miraculous laboratory of thought, whence well up guidances, impulses, intuitions, those things which make the man. Thus though Noorna has gone, Shibli Bagarag has with him as her representative the Talking Hawk. For the present he has ceased to think of his ambition, but his ambition is, so to speak, thinking for him — flashing forth in his need warnings, admonitions, sparks of guidance. The swift pouncing swoop of the hawk finely symbolises these sparks of guidance, abrupt and warning gleams of intuition. By the subtle manner in which they are associated with Noorna we have suggested to us a noble art, no less than the art whereby each man may summon to himself a guardian angel, have it with him in his need. A great love, a passionate ambition is omnipresent. When not in a man's consciousness it is yet effectively behind it, flashing reproof upon him in his errancy, and guidance in his doubt. As a good angel it takes lodgment in his soul, keeping watch and guard there that he lapse not into disloyalty. This privilege pertains to passionate love, earnest ambition of every sort. When Noorna departs, as from time to time she must, she does not leave herself without witness. The Talking Hawk, the Socratic δαίμων takes her place.

As has been said taking ship with Karaz is merely symbolical expression

of the fact that Shibli Bagarag's vanity
has led him astray. He is saved, yet so
as by shipwreck. How otherwise could
he be saved? Woe to a vain man who
prospers in his ways. Vanity overfed
on success becomes little to be distin-
guished from insanity; but in failure
there is wholesome medicine. Scarcely
could a thoroughly successful man,
were there any such, enter the Kingdom
of Heaven; for though the Kingdom
be infinitely wide and high, the en-
trance door is low; one must stoop
and humble himself in order to pass.
We would all be lost but for our failures; it is in the shipwreck of our lives
that we find opportunity of salvation.
Therefore it is that God continually
thwarts us to bless us, stands up against
us that we rush not presumptuously to
our ruin.

When Christian went off the path
his penalty was to fall into the hands
of Giant Despair, and to be kept pris-
oner in Doubting Castle. Shibli Bagarag's penalty for similar errancy was
to flounder, well nigh unto drowning,
in the waters. Meredith's symbolism is
richer than Bunyan's, and has the merit

of being Biblical. The consciousness
of sin takes the solid ground from
under a man, makes him welter, toss,
struggle amid a jumble of doubts, fears,
despondencies. He is like a drowning
man, his supports gone, his wild struggles to right himself but plunging him
deeper under the waters. Bunyan's
symbolism for this state of mind is
lifeless, artificial, as compared with
Meredith's. Neither — and here also the
two Allegorists are giving symbolical
expression to substantially the same
truth — is the key by which Christian
delivered himself from imprisonment to
be counted equal for suggestiveness to
the description of the Hawk supporting
Shibli Bagarag in the waters, holding
him up by the Hair, the Identical. In
Shibli Bagarag's case, any man's case,
the Identical must be taken to represent
that something which is the ultimate
reality, the root-strength of his nature.
Many supports, many faiths man may
have in his easy, normal hours; but
in moments of extremity these, in so
far as they are superficial, vanish, and
the root-faith, the basal strength of his
nature is what he leans on. That root

faith, whatever it be, is the Identical. When all else is gone it is by that he is buoyed up, supported in the waters. Men often mistake the fashions they affect for the faiths they hold, but not during an experience in the waters. In shipwreck they discover their Identical. A man can never carry his heart with him into the barren realms of agnosticism. He may profess a know-nothing attitude towards the mystery of things, but his heart, being itself the mirror and epitome of that mystery, bursts mockingly upon him with its stores of ungotten knowledge. Even the agnostic has thus a faith which his intellect, labour suicidally as it likes, cannot destroy. He also is held up in the waters by his Identical.

The wonders performed by Shibli Bagarag in his interview with the King of Oolb are readily understandable in the light of explanations now given. The interview is notable mainly for the shave which the youth was permitted to give King and courtiers. By his Paravidic eloquence he managed to convince the King that change with respect to Shagpatian fashions was imminent, that a new and happier era for barbercraft was due. The King, be it noted, did not trouble to enquire whether this change would be for the better. His one point of policy was to support the winning side; his one point of genius to discover a day in advance of the world what the winning side was to be. Since barbercraft was destined to be in the ascendant the King then and there had himself shaved. It was a great matter for Shibli Bagarag — a mighty furtherance to his quest after the Ideal — this shave of King and court of Oolb. So limited are the powers of man that he can seldom be quite sure in regard to the changes he advocates how far they would work for good, until he sees them, studies them in operation. Thought needs the verification of fact, must give birth to fact before it can estimate its own value. Actual experiments in reform are invariably necessary to make clear to the reformer the real meaning and drift of his work. Shibli Bagarag is therefore in educative surroundings. He is between the old and the new, the unshaved and the shaved; has opportunity of comparing them, studying the nature and effects of the shave, and so arriving at a clearer conception of his Ideal — his shaved Shagpat. Meredith read deeply into the reality of things when he brought Shibli Bagarag to the City of Oolb in his quest of the Lily.

Reference has already been made to the fact that men who succeed in banishing any tyranny of lies from the world have generally at one period of their lives themselves been under that tyranny; that indeed it is in the process of emancipating themselves that they emancipate the world. In that part of the Allegory entitled "The Flashes of the Blade" we have an account of how Shibli Bagarag liberated the world: in the story of his relations with Princess Goorelka, and his plucking the Lily, we have an account of how he liberated himself. Noise, commotion enough, as will be seen, there was in the objective side of his work — liberating the world. The emancipation of his own thought was conducted without observation. The China jar of wine which drugged the sentinels, and the dress of Samarcand which rendered Shibli Bagarag

invisible, symbolise the fact that the
process of thought emancipation is in
itself a secret process. But if carried
on by itself it would soon also become
an arrested process. It is impossible
to continue to receive light unless one
is at the same time trying to impart it.
Giving is the price of getting; teaching
the condition of learning. Hence neither
the China jar nor the dress of Samarcand could save such a youth as Shibli
Bagarag from detection. All that is
meant is that his quest, in so far as
it was purely subjective, did not itself
lay him open to detection. He attained
unto light quietly; it was when he at-
tempted to spread the light that there
was noise.

Soon as Shibli Bagarag had plucked
the Lily behold the beautiful Goorelka
shrivelled into ugliness, and Noorna —
that still uncomely one — burst on his
enraptured eyes "a young perfection,"
"the very dream of loveliness." It
will be enough to state that Goorelka's
beauty may be taken to represent the
fascination which, owing to false standards of taste, erroneous social ideals,
the Shagpat superstition exercised over

men. On that interpretation Noorna, the negation of Goorelka, must in this connection and in respect of her ugliness, represent the abhorrence with which society viewed the idea of non-hairiness. Fashion rules the world's thinking as tyrannically as the world's tailoring, and fashion had decreed that Goorelka alone was beautiful. For a time Shibli Bagarag was led by the fashion. Youth is necessarily receptive. It drinks in with easy unquestioning faith the opinions and prejudices of the age. But being destined to great things, Shibli Bagarag early began to put the world through the sieve of thought. While yet gazing fascinated on the face of Goorelka the Talking Hawk began to shriek disapproval, the intuitions of his soul to prophesy diviner beauty. By following enquiringly, though still fascinated, on the track of the false — trailing behind Goorelka through the Enchanted Sea — he at length came upon the Lily. The attainment of an independent standard of judgment set him free from conventional standards. The fashion-ridden world might continue to proclaim

Goorelka beautiful; him at least it could no longer deceive. He stood on the hill-tops of life, fronting the light of God, seeing Goorelka and Noorna as they were.

This happy transformation of Noorna is a great matter for Shibli Bagarag. It means that his inward struggle is over, that he is now in a position to throw himself whole-heartedly into the work of shaving Shagpat. It is seen to be such noble, world-helping work that, despite its difficulties and dangers, he cannot but be in love with it. Noorna may still bring him thwacks, but for the joy of being betrothed to such a beauty, he will count thwacks a small matter. Shibli Bagarag has attained unto light. His Ideal has burst upon him in its beauty, and Noorna — as personifying the effort to realise the Ideal — has become correspondingly beautiful. It was long before Luther fully grasped his Lily — his Ideal of a Reformed Church. But when he did his Noorna also burst into beauty. His battle with Rome no longer meant a battle with himself. In respect to that Luther was henceforth at peace, could only be at peace in the midst of war.

Karaz, the enchanted ass, conveyed Shibli Bagarag to the Well of Paravid: the cockle-shell of Goorelka conveyed him to the Lily of the Enchanted Sea. In that there lie several fruitful parallels and contrasts. Enough here to state that what is next door to the truth is never a vacuum but a falsehood. Activity of thought, though thought should be erroneous, is better than absence of thought, for truth, while it may dispossess error, never dispossesses emptiness. So with worship, which is merely the heart's recognition of truth. Better than to have no Ideal is it to trail fascinated after a false one; for the earnestly worshipping eye is after all the deeply enquiring one, and to such truth comes.

Everything in this beautiful and wonderful description of the Enchanted Sea and the Lily therefore is significant. But little further interpretation is required. For this Enchanted Sea is to none of us an unfamiliar Sea. We have ourselves, even the least poetic of us, sailed thereon, perhaps even plucked one of its Lilies. Would we know whether the Lily of our plucking is worthless flower or potent spell? Then let us see to its root. Shibli Bagarag's Lily had for its root a living, palpitating heart. Many flowers, similar maybe in appearance, have for their root nothing better than somnolent, ill-fed brains. Only Lilies with heart for root are Spells acknowledged in Aklis. An Ideal which lives merely in the intellect is a scheme, a theory, an airy and unfruitful speculation. An Ideal which is rooted in and fed by the heart is a masterful power, compelling to action.

But perhaps we leave our Lily unplucked, content ourselves with drinking its dew. Shibli Bagarag was about to succumb to this temptation when the watchful Hawk pounced on the proffered hand of temptress Goorelka, scattering the dew, and screaming this reproof: "Pluck up the Lily ere it is too late O Fool!—the dew was poison. Pluck it by the root with thy right hand." Clearly the temptation here was to treat the Ideal in dilettante fashion, to suck its sweets, rave, enthuse over its beauty—and nothing more. When a man makes noble thought minister to his self-indulgence, when he broods idly, for the sweetness it brings him, on what is beautiful and sublime, he is but poisoning his own soul. The poison is subtle, hard to be detected. Man is apt to think that he is serving God because he enthuses over the things of God; that he is religious because he luxuriates in the sweets of religion. Truly self-indulgence in regard to noble things is subtlest, hardest to be detected of poisons, but deadly poison none the less. Be practical with your Ideal. Pluck the Lily "by the root with thy right hand." The dew that is in it — the sweets of sentimentalism, of enthusing, philandering — are poisoned sweets. May the Talking Hawk be with you in your need to teach you that!

H

THE SWAY OF RABESQURAT

SPECULATION.

ALLEGORY divests life's experiences of their time and space
relations, and rearranges them
according to their thought relations.
The law of association is ignored, the
deeper law of spiritual affinity takes its
place. In the light of this principle the
time order in which these three Spells
were acquired must be discounted.
Doubtless the basal Spell was insight
into facts, and in making it the first to
be acquired Meredith may be considered
true not only to the order of logic, but
to some extent even to that of time.
But practically the quest of all three
Spells was pursued simultaneously.

It is manifest that they are genuine
Spells, that the Allegory is broad-based
on the truth of things. Insight — accurate knowledge of things as they are:
Idealism — clear vision of things as they
ought to be: Enthusiasm — strength to

change things as they are into things
as they ought to be — can it be denied
that these, no more and no less, are
the spells needed for success, whatever
be the sphere of man's activity? It is
not, of course, the worker's tools which
these spells symbolise; it is merely
the skill to properly handle his tools.
But the skill is everything since God
is glad to avail himself of all the
talent there is. If incompetent workmen compete for work, work, in return,
competes for competent workmen.

But the candidate for greatness is not
yet great. He has the spells indeed,
but as yet he has put them to no important use. There is no notable work
to his credit. Were his career to end
at this stage, he would, at best be num-
bered among the brilliant possibilities,
the great might-have-beens of life. But
history has no room, nor has nature
a crown for the might-have-beens. On
then Shibli Bagarag, swift and sure as
arrow from bow, to claim the Sword
and complete the shave. Do something,
be crowned with an achievement, Master of an Event; then indeed you will
be great, God and man acknowledging

your greatness. But hacks that are always on the trot never win races; and men who do n't know the art of rational idleness never attain unto mellow humanity. Shibli Bagarag is going to linger awhile on the Enchanted Sea — the realm of imagination — to dream dreams. Do n't count the study of dreams necessarily a vain study. Even the irresponsible dreams of sleep may play a great part in life, thrust themselves in among realities, twist and turn them with necromantic power. And as for day-dreams, are they not the origin and breeding ground alike of man's baseness and nobility? All his life-history is foreshadowed in his dreams. "Out of the heart are the issues of life"; hence in day-dreams, the unchecked wellings up of the heart, the inmost key to human character is to be found. Know what a man's imagination revels in, what his thoughts, when off the chain, scamper back to, and you know the inmost secret of the man. Also in relation to the world, man is a creator in virtue of being a dreamer. It is not only that every fact was once a fancy, that all that is

realised on earth was once in air, but
that to the last, the root, the essence of
every actuality remains a dream. When
the root withers, when the dream vanishes, the actuality is on the way back
to primitive nothingness. Certainly
then the study of dreams need not be a
vain study.

Consider a noble dream that came to
Shibli Bagarag on the Enchanted Sea.

Less even than other parts of the
Allegory can the story of Noorna and
the Genie Karaz bear prosaic thoroughness of interpretation. It is essentially
a dream-story, a fabric of visionary
thought. This is manifest from the
nature of the story itself, but Meredith
gives additional guidance. The story
was related by Noorna as she and her
betrothed sailed the Enchanted Sea on
a "pearly Shell." This shell — as being
the gift of Rabesqrat, Queen of Illusions — necessarily itself represented an
illusion. As such it is not to be taken
as something different from, but merely
as outward symbol of Shibli Bagarag's
dream — the indication that it was a
dream. Dreams indeed are the only
vessels on which man floats over the

SPECULATION

Enchanted Sea, and this noble dream-vessel, this "pearly shell flashing crimson, amethyst and emerald" finely symbolises the noble dream dreamed by Shibli Bagarag thereon. The case with him was that under the glamour of a freshly-gotten Idealism, lighting up life to him with new meanings, he proved fruitful in speculations, excursions of thought. His reason turned dreamer, and the result was Philosophy; for what is Philosophy but the dream of reason? It is not however the Philosophy of the schools, or anything resembling it we have here. Its kinship rather is with the Philosophy of the seer; for seers also, in respect that their dreams are dreams of reason, must be said to have their Philosophy. But reason with them is in extatic condition — subject so to illuminations, inspirations, visitings of God, but subject also, unless in special guidance, to disturbing and chaotic influences. The prophet's dream may flash forth wondrous truth, but in form it is seldom other than broken, incoherent, irrational. Shibli Bagarag's dream is of this nature. Its three outstanding symbolical characters are Noorna, Karaz and Goorelka; and in regard to none of them is it possible to define their symbolism. It is not a matter of mere inability to give them precise labelling; that, as being more or less a feature of the Allegory throughout, would call for no comment. What is meant is that the characters here are practically indeterminate. They represent simply what Meredith chooses for the occasion to make them represent. He heaps thoughts incongruously upon them, and so naïve is he, so apparently unconscious of the incongruity, as to compel the conviction that the atmosphere of the story is a dream-atmosphere. It is by treating it as a dream, not boggling over incoherences and incongruities, but accepting contentedly such gleams of meaning as it offers, that interpretation becomes possible. I give what seems the general significance of the story.

Noorna and Goorelka, here as always, are opposites. They stand respectively for right and wrong relationship to Karaz—him in whom resides the Power, the Magical Hair. Goorelka, by means of the Ring, is the first to gain power over Karaz. She uses her power wickedly, transforming men into singing birds, peopling her cage with them. Noorna afterwards also manages to gain possession of the Ring, but she puts the power it brings her to worthier use. First she disenchants the occupants of Goorelka's cage, restoring them to their humanity. Then she pulls the Magical Hair from the head of Karaz, and transplants it in that of Shagpat — him whom she now invites Shibli Bagarag to shave. But Goorelka has her revenge. By sprinkling dust on the petals of the Lily of the Enchanted Sea she robs Noorna of her beauty transforms her into a miracle of ugliness. Such, so far as is necessary for our purpose, is the outline of this amazing story.

Call, if you like, the Magical Hair of Karaz the symbol of a lie; yet its might, perniciousness as lie, lay in its truth. Potent lies are never pure lies, oftener than not they are pure truths gripped in wrong fashion. When, for instance, the egoist grips truth, he turns it into falsehood: even the religion of

unselfishness, as grasped by him, min-
isters to the increase of his selfishness.
The lie of the Magical Hair is some
subtle perversion of truth, fitting so
admirably into the nature of man, that
as unmaterialised idea — on the head of
Karaz — detection is impossible. It
must be embodied in a fact, allowed to
work itself out, unfold its nature in
alliance with fact, before it can be
detected. Hence Noorna, representing
the good power, soon as she gets
control of the Hair, pulls it from the
Genie's head, and plants it in that of
Shagpat. Otherwise put, she plants the
mighty Hair among the facts, that so
working itself out, unfolding its nature,
detection and shaving may follow. The
immediate result of her action is doubtless to increase the unholy power of
the Hair. As unrealised idea — unmaterialised lie — it had held a select body
of visionary fools, occupants of Goorelka's cage, in enchantment. But as
planted on the head of Shagpat — made
a visible dignity, a potent institution —
its power for evil is immeasurably
greater. Nevertheless in this manner,
and in no other, can the world

ultimately free itself from the enchantment of the Hair. Nothing is discredited
until it is discredited by experience.
Slavery, Feudalism, the Divine Right
of Kings — have not these and many
other Magical Hairs held men in the
past in enchantment? And had they
not to work themselves fully out, reveal
by abundant interplay with facts the
falsehood that was in them, before it
was possible to shave them — banish
them from among men? In the world
of to-day, Magical Hairs, many of them,
are working themselves out, revealing
the good or evil which is theirs. Until
the revelation is complete, it is fated
that they hold men in enchantment,
and no power can break the enchantment. Are there not also mighty Hairs
rooted still in the head of Genii — nowhere yet on earth — holding so vision-
aries in enchantment, making them sing
the song of enchantment? Never perhaps was the world more fruitful in
unrealised ideas than at present. Genii
float before its vision carrying mighty
Hairs, potent, each one of them, with
the magic of promise; mightiest of
such being perhaps, for the present,

Socialism. If these Hairs are good, Noorna, the beneficent one, will transplant them — bring them to earth — that men may rejoice in their goodness. If they are bad, she yet in her wisdom may transplant them, that men, discerning their badness, may shave them, rid themselves of enchantment. But truly good and bad mingle meanings here. The good becomes the bad when men cleave to it badly. Even a worthy custom, when adhered to merely as custom, blights the spirit of man. Hence it is that:

"The old order changeth, yielding
   place to new,
And God fulfils himself in
   many ways,
Lest one good custom should
   corrupt the world."

This dream then, if we may still call it so, is reason's dream on Providence, as manifested in the rise and fall of systems and institutions. To enrich human consciousness, unfold spirit unto itself, is the purpose of Providence in history. Hence man is driven through all experiences, but permitted to rest in none. Truth is reached by

him in no other way than by climbing
to it on the back of error; error therefore has place, relative value in the
scheme of things. Noorna brings about
the shaving of Shagpat, yet Noorna
also it was who planted the Magical
Hair on Shagpat. Buildings up and
pullings down are alike of God.

The interpretation now given will be
found to fit into, shed light upon most
of the intricacies of the story. Apply
it for example to the Ring which gave
command of the Magical Hair on the
head of Karaz. In terms of our interpretation the Ring must be taken to
mean approximately knowledge. Knowledge is mastery. The power of delusion lies in that men do n't know it to
be delusion. Once come to know, and
the Ring gives them power over the
Hair. But power only while it remains
on the head of Karaz. On the head of
Shagpat it is no longer under but a
"contradiction to the power of the
Ring." That is to say, knowledge gives
mastery over delusion merely as delusion. But to the extent that delusion
is materialised, embodied among the
facts of life, made say a powerful

institution, knowledge in itself gives no mastery. The Hair of Error then sets itself in opposition to, stubbornly battles against the Ring of Knowledge. When Rome made it her policy to suppress such enlightenment as threatened to endanger her supremacy, when she struggled to confine the thought of Christendom to grooves prescribed by herself — it was the Hair acting in "contradiction to the power of the Ring." And though chosen spirits continually brought the Ring of Knowledge to bear on that Hair of Error, little practical good was effected. The Ring enabled them to see the error but not to abolish it; gave them mastery over it in the abstract — as on the head of Karaz, but left them impotent toward it in the concrete — as on the head of Shagpat. Hence the fallacy — as applicable to Rome in her power — of that saying of Erasmus: "Spread the light and darkness will vanish of itself." Translated into allegorical language the saying meant that since the Ring had power over the Hair on the head of Karaz, it must also have power over it on the head of Shagpat. Or, giving it another allegorical translation, it meant that provided that Shagpat's Hair was lathered sufficiently, it would by miraculous process, and without touch of razor, shave itself. It is not so the world's errors are abolished. Everything is to be fought with on its own plane of being. What is purely spiritual is to be overcome, can indeed be overcome, by none save spiritual weapons — nought save the Ring can master the Hair on the head of Karaz. But when a thing is at once spiritual and material, then on both planes of being must battle with it be waged. Lathering must industriously be attended to, but after the lathering must come the Sword.

It is by reference to a change in the standards of taste that the loss of beauty which befell Noorna through Goorelka casting dust on the petals of the Lily is to be explained. Beauty is in the eye that sees it. What is lovely in the eyes of one age or people may be loathsome in the eyes of another. The case with Noorna simply was that as Shagpat brought hairiness into fashion, she as representing non-hairiness

I

had to go out of fashion. It was she who brought the Magical Hair to earth — that being the only way by which men might ultimately free themselves of its magic. But while the magic holds, while public taste continues vitiated, Noorna must appear ugly. She thus, as representing the good power, accepts voluntary martyrdom for the sake of the world. 'Tis by this way of voluntary martyrdom that goodness achieves all its victories; the cross is the universal emblem and method of its power. In the Gospel is thus found the central truth, which is also the central mystery, of the moral universe.

These and other glimpses of profoundest thought will reward those who study this portion of the Allegory carefully. Enough has here been said by way of general interpretation.

ILLUSION

NEVER is Karaz so dangerous as when he haunts the Enchanted Sea in the form of fish. Could he be altogether excluded from these Waters, kept from infesting and polluting the imagination of man, small damage could he work. But while man sails Karaz will swim the Enchanted Sea, preying on souls.

But behold how there may be protection from Karaz, the shark that preys on souls. Open mouthed comes the monster to devour Shibli Bagarag as he sails the Sea in the "pearly shell" of his noble dream. But Noorna, the wise one, hurriedly closes the shell, shutting her betrothed up in it, so protecting him from evil. For as he descends into that unholy place — the belly of the fish — he hears "outside the shell a rushing, gurgling noise, and a noise as of shouting multitudes and

123

muffled multitudes, muttering complaints and yells and querulous cries."
'T was the echo of the world in its sordidness, the babel-cry of its battlings and graspings of greed, the multitudinous noise of life's weary whirl of illusions, "sound and fury signifying nothing" that Shibli Bagarag heard in the belly of the fish. Well for him that 't was as an echo he heard it, that not even in imagination did he join the sordid scramble. For this thanks are due to Noorna who shut him up in the "pearly shell" of his noble thought, sheltering him so from baseness. A noble thought is the soul's defensive armour; encased in it a man may suffer bombardment from life's pollutions and take no stain. "The whole armour of God"—if in the urgency of battle you forget its details, take it just as the "pearly shell" of a noble thought. Shut yourself up in that shell, but not alone, for an academic thought, however noble, is poor defence against the Evil One. Let Noorna, Duty, be with you as companion, and then though in the belly of Karaż, you are safe from pollution. This Allegory is to be placed

alongside that of the Talking Hawk, as finely illustrating another aspect of the saving power of thought.

But further danger, from which escape is not so speedy, awaits Shibli Bagarag in the Enchanted Sea. It is symbolised by his sojourn in the Realm of Rabesqurat.

In descending from the House Beautiful to the Valley of Humiliation Christian "caught a slip," and in consequence had to encounter Apollyon in the valley. Shibli Bagarag is in similar condition. He too has been on the heights, had vision of the Ideal — to him indeed the House Beautiful — and now in getting back to himself, resuming the prosaic activities of life, he too catches a slip. His encounter with Rabesqurat is at once the consequence and the emblem — the allegorical presentation — of his slip. It is primarily a slip into vain anticipation. In place of settling down to the task of realising his ideal, he gives way to day-dreams, indolent anticipations of its realisation. Were it merely a case of looking hopefully forward to the time when Shagpat would be shaved, no fault would be his.

But it is more than that. It is a case
of dreamily imagining that the deed is
actually done, the world showering
honours on him the doer. Day-dreams
are romances in which every man is
his own hero; and, fittingly enough,
Shibli Bagarag's thoughts seem to have
been on the glorious condition of himself, scarcely at all on the happy condition of the world under a shaved
Shagpat. The case with him thus
was that in descending from the House
Beautiful to actual life he breaks his
journey, dwells for a time in a castle-
in-the-air. He would be an over-rigid
moralist who altogether condemned
castles-in-the-air, for surely these fairy
habitations may on occasion prove san-
itoria, places of health and healing for
the confined and overwrought spirit.
None the less to linger long in them is
ever to run great risk. In Shibli Bagarag's case the risk was that he came
near losing the key of his castle, being
imprisoned there for life. His day dream
proved terribly persistent. It clung
about him, held him in such sweet
fetters, that he could scarcely break
away. It was only by using violence

126

on himself that he at last summoned strength to smash the enchanted halls of Rabesqurat, and make his escape.

In direct line of the story Shibli Bagarag's sojourn in the realm of Rabesqurat thus primarily symbolises on his part the revelling in vain anticipation, dreaming his great task into completion rather than working to make it so. But to stop here would be to give the Allegory a misleadingly inadequate interpretation. As general description of man's condition of soul under indolent dreams, it bears a meaning not different from, but wider, more comprehensive than that now given. The enervating, will-weakening effect of day-dreams, the manner in which they make man blunder among, misconstrue the facts of life, is subtly portrayed. By the pathway of vain anticipation indeed it is that Shibli Bagarag enters the realm of Rabesqurat, but, the floodgates of folly once open, he is betrayed unto himself, pitilessly buffeted by his own weakness, so losing his spiritual treasure, the Lily. That notable loss must necessarily be considered, but since to follow other details would involve a lengthy study, I can only endeavour suggestively to cover them by a redescription, couched in sufficiently general terms, of Shibli Bagarag's condition of soul.

It may be said to have been a condition due to that law of reaction which affects all human activity. The bow unbends. The native indolence of human nature asserts itself. Shibli Bagarag was weary. That passion for reality which had ennobled him, singled him out from the crowd, was for the time being spent. Why probe continually beneath appearances? Why neglect the present good, struggling after far-off ideals? Were it not better to take life as it is, daintily skimming the surface of things?

"Death is the end of life — ah! why
    Should life all labour be?

These, be it noted, were not questions deliberately put and answered by Shibli Bagarag. The realm of Rabesqurat is the realm, not of deliberation, but of *drifting*. The reformer allowed Noorna to be taken from him, but he did not himself put her away. There was no abandonment of his ambition, but other interests — life's pleasures and relaxations — intervened for a time between him and it. The case with Shibli Bagarag thus merely was that he paused "wearied in the greatness of his way." The pause might have proved fatal. The rudder of his will, hitherto inflexibly held, being let go, the man began to dangerously drift. Indolence, spiritual lethargy, a sleepy shrinking from the real, an unwillingness to shatter pleasant dreams — that constituted his weakness and Rabesqurat's strength. "He assisted in beguiling himself." "He was as one that slideth down a hill and can arrest his descent with a foot, yet faileth that free will." Realities were unrelenting, unflattering, thwack-bringing ; wearily, petulantly he thrust them aside. Dreams were soothing, plastic, tickling to vanity; ah! let his soul have holiday — let him drift and dream and be at ease. The great man had forgotten his greatness ; Rabesqurat, Queen of Illusions, befooled him for a time.

Whom has not the terrible Queen befooled? Most men alas, not for a time, but for the whole unfruitful length of their days linger idling in her realm, slaves of illusion, fatally yet consentingly befooled. They have spells, all of them, similar in kind, if not in potency, to Shibli Bagarag's — spells sufficient at least to free them from the Queen's worst enchantments. But though man is strong he is not master of his strength. Though he is wise he neglects his wisdom. The God in him sleeps. Queen Rabesqurat has her will. From delusion unto delusion mortal man is tossed. Verily his life is a "vain show."

Meredith's aim, in this part of the Allegory, is not so much to inform us respecting the particular temptations which assailed Shibli Bagarag as to describe the condition of soul which laid him open to temptation at all. Nature abhors a vacuum, but Satan delights in one. He is the Lord of Empty Places. Shibli Bagarag. gave way to idleness, let his mind be empty, and at once Satan was at him with his foul magic, befooling him, dozing him with illusions, making his senses traitors to his soul. It does not appear however that the youth abandoned

himself even in thought to any grossness. For this no thanks to his self-
control; at the time he was exercising
none. His better self was dozing unto
sleep, but happily his fair heredity, his
wholesome instincts — the self within
the self — stood his good angel while
he slept, guarding him from baser evils.
It was at the worst a case of spiritual
backsliding, lapsing into worldliness —
worldly mindedness — with the youth.
Not even in imagination did he abandon himself to grossness, but the
shows, the vanities, the pomp and pride
of life ensnared his heart. 'T was a
condition in which all his spells were
deteriorating through lack of use. But
the noblest is ever the first to suffer,
the readiest to feel the blight of neglect. Hence the loss of the Lily. Lest
my former interpretation should have
lacked in explicitness let me here state,
though surely it is sufficiently evident,
that this Lily, the Ideal, is more than
an intellectual concept, more than
Shibli Bagarag's vision of what ought
to be, of what as reformer he is struggling to achieve. As rooted in the heart
it is a very personal matter. Call it if

you like "the white flower of a blameless life," purity, goodness, spirituality — no one name fully describes it. The light granted to the pure in heart is what the Light of this Lily accurately is, and 't is a light which serves a man not only to work by but to live by, at once guiding his activities and shining in upon himself, flooding his soul with joy. This divinest treasure Shibli Bagarag lost as Christian lost his "Roll" — with which by the way it may be profitably compared — because of his "sinful sleep." Were man awake he could keep God company even in the realm of Rabesqurat; were he altogether awake indeed it would be no realm of Rabesqurat for him. But something less than that is desirable. It is the part of wisdom to treat Rabesqurat guardedly yet complacently, to keep, while passing through her realm, defensive grip of one's spells; but not to use them for the gratuitous exposure of the Queen. The wise man knows Rabesqurat to be illusion, but he knows also that even as illusion she has meaning and value. But that is a wisdom hard to attain unto. To most men the realm of Rabesqurat is the realm of sleep, forgetfulness. Whether amid the austerities of the desert or the gaieties of the city, he who sleeps, forgets his better-self — his spells — is in slavery to Rabesqurat. It is a slavery hard to be avoided. So terribly does the outward fight against the inward that to yield oneself even for a little to the shows and witcheries of sense is to be in danger of that loss of spiritual vision which is slavery. For as the Teacher says:

"Ye that the inner spirit's sight
would seal
Nought credit but what outward
orbs reveal."

"The soul of Shibli Bagarag was blinded by Rabesqurat in the depth of the Enchanted Sea," hence the Ideal, which is the seeing of the soul, was lost. The spiritual in him suffered inanition — what was there in that life of indolence and vanity to feed the spiritual? Yet though Shibli Bagarag was rapidly drifting into worldliness, for a time, so treacherous is the magic of Rabesqurat, he did not know it. It was however misery, remorse, the

133

"bosom of darkness" with him when he came to himself and found the Lily gone. The magic halls of Rabesqurat, erstwhile flashing brilliances, were to him places of gloom, their lamps "swinging lamps without light." While that "Master light of all our seeing" remained quenched in him, no other light might shine. For the Ideal, take it in what sense you will, if the enemy, is yet the friend of the Real. If it shows up the defects of things, it is yet that which gives them their meaning and value. By the light of the Lily Shibli Bagarag saw all that was actual blemish-marked; without the light of the Lily the world was to him wholly a place of darkness, its lamps "swinging lamps without light."

When vision fails do not stand still, but grope. To stand still is to consent to darkness; to grope is to petition for light. Had Shibli Bagarag at that crisis in his career stood still, paralysed with despair, he would have been lost. But this was a youth that never throughout his career was actually *imprisoned* in Doubting Castle. The outward trend of his activities, his happy freedom from ultra introspection, saved him from that danger. The moment he came to himself Shibli Bagarag — in this the type of true repentance — began to grope, sadly yet hopefully, through the darkened halls of Rabesqurat, using — it was all he could do — the lower to guide him to the higher, the Water of Paravid to guide him to the Lily. When formerly he found the Lily it brought him pure joy, but this time, because of his backsliding, agony mingled with the joy. To get it he had to do a terrible thing — pluck the heart out of that awesomely lovely one, the silver-white, radiance-spreading damsel. I shall explain briefly what seems to be the primary meaning of this piercingly beautiful Allegory.

In regard to sacred things it cannot but be that while we are working with them, putting them to practical use, their glory is partly hidden from us. It is manifestly well that this should be so, for were tools to overawe the hand that works with them, they would cease to be tools. Viewed therefore as touchstone of the actual, pattern for remodelling the actual, practical spell of any sort, the Ideal finds its modest but fitting emblem in the Lily. But should man, after a lapse into disloyalty, make painful recovery of the Ideal, it takes on another and an awesome symbolism. No mere model of beauty, aesthetic abstraction, is it known to be then; a sentient being rather, of holiness and anguish unspeakable. The man feels that his sin has gone beyond himself, reached out to the wounding, lacerating the heart of the Holy One. This it is which constitutes the mystery and significance of sin, this instinctive feeling on the part of the sinner that his sin has gone beyond himself, struck at and wounded the heart of Infinite Love. The consciousness of his wrongdoing as it affected himself was to Shibli Bagarag so lost sight of, swallowed up in this larger, terribler consciousness that his heart's cry was the cry of the Psalmist: "Against thee, thee only have I sinned, and done this evil in thy sight." However it be with man's intellect, his heart cannot become vocal without acknowledging God. Stir his heart into prophecy with any profound emotion —

136

provided it be profound it matters little what the emotion — and the prophecy is of God. This significant fact is witnessed to frequently in the Allegory, nowhere more remarkably than in the passage now explained.

This noble Allegory of backsliding, repentance and restoration ought to receive independent study from the reader. I have merely given its primary meaning, the one most directly in line with the story, but so rich is it in the magical qualities of Allegory that fresh meanings and beauties will reveal themselves to every competent seeker.

It would be wrong to leave the realm of Rabesqurat without making acquaintance of little man Abarak "keeper of the Seventh Pillar." More will afterwards appear of the Seventh Pillar, but take it meantime merely to represent the will. Strength, steadfastness of will, is indeed the seventh, the perfect pillar of human nature. Abarak "keeper of the Seventh Pillar" was thus a man of great will power, and in that lay his strength. Yet his limitations in point of intellect made his strength of little avail. So lacking was he in the

J

"seeing eye and the understanding heart" that he lived enmeshed in the toils of Rabesqurat, certain to remain so unless some nobler spirit helped him to freedom. Shibli Bagarag does him this best of services. He opens his eyes to the hollowness of the life he is leading, imparts to him — by means of the Lily — a saving glimpse of nobler things. The little man, recognising in the youth a master spirit, gives himself up to him in loyal servitude; and in such servitude finds his true life.

Beautiful was the relationship thus established between these two "brothers in adventure." It was a relationship based on exchange of spells, mutual helpfulness in noble things. Abarak toiled for, because he could not see through Rabesqurat; Shibli Bagarag toyed with, because he did not wish to see through her. Abarak imparts to Shibli Bagarag his strength, resoluteness — lends him his Bar; Shibli Bagarag imparts to Abarak his insight, spiritual vision — lends him his Lily; and so leaning on each other, the twain pass on to achievement.

ILLUSION

Some things there may be that a wise man will not lend to another, but his spells he ought always to lend. He runs no risk of losing them in the lending, rather they come back to him enriched. God has placed us in society in order to establish a great Human Stock Exchange — spells being the stock exchanged. Happy he who transacts much business in this Exchange; there is service in it, and 't is a service "twice blessed, it blesseth him that gives and him that takes."

VANITY

IT must already be apparent that
the different regions through which
Shibli Bagarag travelled were but
different aspects of one region, human
life viewed from different points of
view. Shagpatism represents life in
its institutional aspect, full of errors,
superstitions and wrongs. The Quest
of the Spells represents life in its aspiring and disciplinary aspect, a school
wherein, by much effort and hardship,
man may learn wisdom. The Realm of
Rabesqurat represents life in its frivol-
ous, pleasure-loving, superficial aspect.
Aklis — the region to which Shibli
Bagarag now comes — represents life in
what may be called its legal aspect,
using that word not in its institutional,
but in its cosmic sense. This devil's
lottery of existence, this chaotic tossing
and tumbling of things — see it through
the eye of Aklis and all is order, law,

government. "No aid or friendliness in Aklis." No chance or injustice in Aklis. Here the Unseen Powers keep shop. All manner of merchandise, suiting every taste, is to be got in exchange for spells. But without Spells, appointed and of proportionate value, nothing is to be got, for the Unseen Powers are strict merchantmen, and no dispensers of charity.

Aklis is the realm not of efforts, but of results; cursed are they who linger in it. At no time can a man, if true to his manhood, say "I have done enough. I will rest on my laurels, and take my reward." Men with a future before them pass through Aklis, claiming the Sword, the Bar, whatever weapon their spells can purchase. Men who have outlived their ambition and are content with their achievements settle down in Aklis, nestle in it, make it their home. They are under a curse — these last. Past achievements, however great, are not a capital, on the reputation of which, as on interest, a man can live honourably idle. To cease seeking great things is to cease being great.

To Shibli Bagarag Aklis appeared

VANITY

"a strange, dusky land, as it seemed a
valley, on one side of which was a
ragged copper sun setting low. . . . . .
The sky was a brown colour; the earth
a deeper brown, like the skins of tawny
lions." Sparkle, brightness, glint of
living light was there none in Aklis.
The description is significant. Nothing
in life is so disenchanting as its results.
The spirit of hope, which is the spirit
of poetry, lights with some touch of
living light earth's dreariest realm of
effort; but over the realm of results
there broods dullness, the prosaic spirit.
A man can be mocked by his failures
and yet keep in love with life, but woe
to him who is mocked by his successes.
Happily it can be said success mocks
no man until he attempts to rest in it;
then indeed it deservedly mocks him.

It is generally by way of the Enchanted Sea of anticipation that man
enters the rich but sombre realm of
results, and the realm suffers unduly
by the contrast. Mayhap, however,
Shibli Bagarag carries with him a phial
of water from this Enchanted Sea, and
that on occasion he will pour drops
from it on the sombre things of Aklis,

causing them, not indeed to speak, but to glisten, dance and sing. He is a likely youth to have such a phial in his possession. But for the present he has disported himself sufficiently with enchantments; 't is good that for a period he should stand clear of them, look out on life in practical, prosaic mood.

Consider his experiences in this realm.

Through the Palace of Aklis — the mart of the world — he passes, beholding, estimating its wealth of wares. Just here many mighty ones, "brothers in adventure" have closed ignominiously their careers, making fool's barter of their hard-won spells. The youth's love for Noorna, his native cleanliness of spirit, carry him unsmirched through life's grosser temptations. Neither avarice nor sensual pleasures conquer him. Those whom they conquer, Meredith, with fine scorn, describes as monstrosities, half-human, half-bestial in form, not passers through but wolfish, swinish settlers in Aklis. But Shibli Bagarag's own fall, a hurtful one, awaits him in the Hall of the

144

VANITY

Duping Brides. To understand its nature
be it said that by this time he has attained unto a certain measure of fame.
It is known that he has the three
mighty Spells, and that in consequence
he is likely to come to great things.
Men worship the rising sun; and this
youth, famous and growing in fame,
has naturally all sorts of people buzz-
ing about him, flattering him. His fall
comes through their flatteries, or rather
through that vanity in him to which
their flatteries make appeal. And
here note the prophetic quality of day-
dreams. In the realm of Rabesqurat —
imagination — Shibli Bagarag's dreams,
foolish though they were, had in them
no taint of grossness. They were
vanity-inspired dreams, revellings in
imaginary fame. His actual life proved
but a replica of his dream-life. The
first and second temptations in Aklis
— temptations to grossness — were to
him scarcely temptations at all. But
the third temptation, as making appeal
to his vanity, proved irresistible. "Out
of the heart are the issues of life."
The day-dream foreshadows the reality.
The case with Shibli Bagarag in the

Hall of the Duping Brides thus merely is that he is entangled in his own weakness. Sweet to him is this novel but long-looked for experience of popular applause, yea for the sweetness of it he is as one "in the midst of a very rose-garden of young beauties, such as the Blest behold in Paradise." He feels himself one of nature's kings, exalted, crowned with fame; for a crown, and no less, is what these Brides — symbolising by their beauty and blandishments the sweetness of fame — seem to offer him. But the youth is on his guard, or tries to be. Thrice already in his experience has he been saluted as king, and "till now it was a beguilement, all emptiness." Therefore though his "head itcheth for the symbols of majesty" he will first test the honesty of these Brides by his two hitherto trustworthy tests — the Water of Paravid and the Light of the Lily. They blink, water in the eyes a little, but — Duping Brides though they are — stand the test sufficiently well. Are his spells at fault then at last? Why not? They are not objective things — these spells, but merely symbols of the youth's spiritual con-

dition — his clearness of vision, purity
of heart; hence they necessarily find
their limit in contact with what remains
in him of weakness, especially when,
as it happens, vanity is his weakness.
For the nature of vanity is that while
it reveals itself to all the world, it hides
itself from its own possessor. When a
man is vain everybody is likely to
know it sooner than himself. Shibli
Bagarag indeed has bruised himself too
frequently against his own vanity to
be altogether ignorant of its existence.
But his knowledge, as being neither
humble nor watchful, is no better than
ignorance. He is one to admit that he
is vain, and to smile vainly at the ad-
mission. Therefore it is that his spells
prove at fault here, or rather — putting
it more correctly — that he proves at
fault in the application of them. He
uses them to test the innocence of
the Brides' blandishments, whereas he
ought to have used them to test
whether he could with impunity stand
their blandishments. The Brides' blandishments — as symbolising popular applause — were not insincere. Crowds
never flatter. There is always sincerity

in the applause of the multitude.
Shallow, short-lived, and of little
worth their favor may be, but for the
moment at least it is genuine. In that
respect the Water of Paravid did not
report falsely. On the larger question
as to the value of fame in itself, it
could scarcely be expected to report
impartially. Such report as it gives,
that is to say such reflections on the
subject as Shibli Bagarag could attain
unto, are described with large poetic
freedom in the charming snatches of
verse which the Brides are made to
utter. If you judge from these snatches
of verse that the impassioned and ambitious youth overestimates the joys of
fame — the urgency with which it ought
to be pursued; judge also whether in
your phlegmatic wisdom you may not
as likely be underestimating them. But
indeed Shibli Bagarag faces the whole
question conscientiously, striving to be
thorough with himself. It is not only
the Water of Paravid but the Lily — the
moral test — he applies to the Brides.
Can he pursue fame without damage
to his better self — take joy in it and
yet be blameless in the sight of God?

VANITY

Allowing that the question was too personal to be debated altogether impartially, that some measure of the inevitable prejudice in favour of self must have broken in upon his deliberations, can it be said that he came to a wrong conclusion? Surely it is not sin to take pleasure in the approval of one's fellows; were one indeed not to do so would it not but argue in him the lack of healthy social instincts? To stoop to unworthiness through greed of popularity is indeed great sin; but when fame and favour come in the pursuit of duty a man does well to rejoice in them, to count them among his legitimate rewards. Shibli Bagarag's decision was right. The Brides stand the test of the Lily, if not indeed perfectly, as well at least as most earthly pleasures. For all that they proved but Duping Brides, working shame and danger to Shibli Bagarag. See now the nature of their Duping.

The desire for applause acts as an incentive; applause itself when it comes, tends to act as a soporific. Shibli Bagarag drinks at the cup of his own fame, and the potion sends him

to sleep. His better self, his heroic
self is sound asleep, but to be sure his
vanity-tickled, vain-glorious self is de-
lightedly awake. Because he is the
man of the hour — fêted, lionised, wor-
shipped of the multitude — he jumps to
the conclusion that his dreams of greatness have come true at last. But they
have not come true; they are simply
being duplicated. Shibli Bagarag is
still dreaming; never a sillier, more
hurtful dream has he had than this.
For, and this is the Duping, by fancying himself great he is cheating himself of greatness. No longer intent on
achieving but on enjoying, no longer
struggling to Master an Event, but
revelling in that popularity which he
imagines is the proof and the reward
of Mastery — is he not now among
those base ones who settle down in
Aklis, make it their home? His career
is at a standstill. In relation to his life-
mission he is represented in the Allegory — and note the truth rather than
the irony of the symbolism — as a benumbed and pathetic figure, sitting on
a throne from which he could not
move. Clearly Shibli Bagarag is not

strong enough to stand the Brides'
blandishments. As cheer, encourage-
ment in his work, could he take them
so, they would do him good and not
harm. But he cannot take them so.
The breath of popular applause has
fanned his vanity into a mighty flame,
and in that flame his whole manhood
threatens to be consumed. Alas for the
erstwhile strenuous youth that his head
should be turned, his time wasted in
this silliest fashion. One's first loving
wish is that a shower of lusty thwacks,
thwacks of the old stinging quality,
could once again be apportioned him.
But what good would they be likely
to do? Vanity, when grown great, feeds
and flourishes on all things. If applause
is what fattens it, reproach and hisses
are what strengthen it, give it muscle.
Had it been possible for the world to
thwack Shibli Bagarag into humility,
verily by this time he had been humble.
But for this more searching thwacks
than the world's are required, and,
praise the Disposer of Destinies! the
administering of them at last begins.
As Shibli Bagarag sat on that benumbing throne "his gaze fell on a mirror,

and he beheld the crown on his forehead what it was, bejewelled asses' ears,
stiffened upright, and the skulls of
monkeys grinning with gems. The
sight of that crowning his head con-
vulsed Shibli Bagarag with laughter,
and as he laughed his seat upon the
throne was loosened, and he pitched
from it." The mirror in which Shibli
Bagarag thus saw himself was the
mirror of self-consciousness; his laughter the bitter laughter of self-criticism.
Of all the furniture of the human
spirit count this mirror among the most
precious, for truly its qualities of wonder are inexhaustible. Morbidity comes
to him who looks at it too much; folly
accumulates on him who looks at
it too little; wisdom would be his who
looked at it aright. It is a mirror to
liberate all whom it makes laugh.
Laughter is the emotion of reason, the
channel by which, under shock of
surprise, reason relieves its feelings.
When it is a man's self that gives his
reason a surprise, the pealing of his
laughter is but the screaming of his
self-love under the lash. Thwackings
of this nature bring liberation to the

soul. The man who cannot laugh at himself is in bondage to himself. The man who cannot see over his own shoulder will never grow taller. Self-criticism is the chief saving grace of life; that it lose not this dignity see that it be practised in no pettifogging spirit. A morbid martinet of a conscience is sore company, and the grace of God is not in it. A wise man forgives himself much.

Shibli Bagarag's first touch of humility comes through the teachings of prosperity. While the world thwacked him his soul hardened itself in pride; now that it smiles on him, he has a saving glimpse of his own unworthiness. He, forsooth, fancying himself one of nature's kings, laying himself out with fine air of majesty to collect the homage of men! The dream — 'twas the silliest of dreams —vanishes in agonies of liberating laughter. Shibli Bagarag is again merely a candidate, be sure a much humbled candidate for greatness. His gain from his folly, his sinful waste of time, is that his vanity has at last made him appear ridiculous in his own eyes, that now therefore

153

K

for the first time he sets himself against it, knows it to be his enemy.

None the less he cannot purge his heart of vanity. The laughter of self-criticism has indeed driven him to break free, for the time being, from the entanglements of popular applause, but it has not killed in him the craving for applause. He resumes the strenuous life — gets off the throne, but he cannot eradicate vanity from his heart — remove the ass-eared crown. That crown "stuck to him, and was tenacious of its hold as a lion that pounceth upon a victim." The prospect is alarming. A reformer must indeed be sensitive to public opinion, since that in the last issue is the weapon by which he accomplishes his reform. But his sensitivity must be of an impersonal nature, no touch of vanity in it. Every popular reformer must count on, be prepared to face unpopularity. But here is Shibli Bagarag setting about the work of reform with a crown of "bejewelled asses' ears, stiffened upright" on his head. The prospect is certainly alarming. In spite of himself he will be listening, straining these asses' ears of his to catch this man's flatteries, that man's abuse — delighted by the one, irritated by the other, influenced by all — till steadiness and the cunning of barbercraft forsake his wrist. If Shibli Bagarag cannot get rid of his crown, he had better put down his razor, for 't is certain he will make a botch of the shave. But patience, for much has already been accomplished. The youth has seen, caught one saving glimpse of himself in the mirror of self-consciousness, and the result already is that the vain one is up in arms against his own vanity, the crowned one tugging indignantly at his crown in effort to tear it off. To man in this condition God's grace is ever available.

DOINGS OF THE SONS OF AKLIS

PURGATION

A KLIS, as being the realm of results, necessarily has its spiritual region, for results may be spiritual as well as material. Few men directly seek spiritual results, but to some extent all men find them, for the by-products of human activity continually tend to be spiritual. Yet to find such results in soul saving measure conscious seeking is necessary. Shibli Bagarag does well therefore in that having discovered the unsatisfying nature of the world's rewards, its pleasures and applause, he aspires to enter the spiritual region of Aklis, in search of true treasure.

Spiritual rewards are ultimate rewards — he who truly finds them knows them to be so. None the less to settle contentedly down, make one's home in even this region of Aklis, is capital offence. Spirituality divorced from

159

constant aspiration is a contradiction in terms. God is the foe of finality. The moment a man thinks he has attained the goal, he is cast back to restart the journey. Spiritual results give way under the man who would rest on them. A special curse therefore is on those who loiter, think to settle down in this region of Aklis. It is the region of divine discontent, and men must enter it seeking not lodgment and Nirvanic ease, but the Sword.

Shibli Bagarag reached this spiritual region by crossing an Abyss on a bridge of Roc's eggs. Of the Roc, dread inhabiter of the Abyss, we are told that it "threatened mankind with ruin," that Aklis, the Father, "subdued it with his Sword" and that a stain of its "blood is yet on the hilt of the Sword." If the Abyss be taken to represent the heart of man, and the Roc to represent sin, or rather that evil principle in man which is the source of sin, the Allegory will reveal its meaning, and in doing so link itself, not for the first time, distinctively on to Christian teaching. Aklis, the Divine One, subduing the Roc of the Abyss — that "evil heart of unbelief"—what can it symbolise, if indeed it has any definite symbolism, but the redeeming labours of Christ, recognition that "God was in Christ reconciling the world unto himself"?

On this interpretation the bridge of Roc's eggs must be taken to represent sins. Sins are the only eggs that evil bird lays. Notice however they were empty eggs — mere shells; how otherwise could Shibli Bagarag have passed through them to the Heavenly Powers? A full egg would have meant a living sin, a sin indulged in and unrenounced; one such would have been barrier indeed. But these hollow eggs were dead sins, sins Shibli Bagarag had cast or was struggling to cast behind him. Therefore since "Men may rise on stepping stones of their dead selves to higher things," it was through the empty eggs of the Roc of the Abyss — literally his dead self — that Shibli Bagarag came into the Presence. As a description of the nature of repentance, the method of moral growth, this Allegory grips truth closely and in richly suggestive fashion. I have here given merely its general meaning; it will repay those who study it in detail.

By the pathway of repentance Shibli Bagarag passes into the presence of the Sons of Aklis, the Heavenly Powers. As symbolical characters these Sons of Aklis must be taken to represent God's dealings, his grace and government in relation to men. But Meredith's symbolical characters, though never other than symbolical, are yet living beings, pulsating with concrete life, playing their part in story as well as allegory. Call these Sons of Aklis, if you like, simply the Heavenly Powers, understanding that term in the sense now given.

Shibli Bagarag enters their presence in penitential mood, renouncing, so far as in him lies, all sin. Could he by mere effort of will cleanse his soul, surely now there would be cleansing. But in the remaking of a man, while everything depends on, nothing seems actually done by the will. That asseared crown — grotesque yet truthful symbol of his greed of flatteries — still sticks to Shibli Bagarag's head; and neither can he remove it, nor while it remains can he hope modestly to govern the ears thereof that they sniff not in applause, tingle with the joy of it. His will is awakened, it is strenuous, it is doing all that will can do; but it cannot reach down into his heart to eradicate therefrom the greed of flatteries. Yet eradicated the greed must be, not only because in practical life it would inevitably betray him into much folly, but because in its own nature it is peculiarly offensive to the Heavenly Powers. Vanity vitiates virtue. Humility is the court-dress of Heaven; virtues which are not "clothed in humility" are forbidden the presence of the King. Shibli Bagarag in a sense is humble enough; the glimpse he caught of himself in the mirror of self-consciousness has sufficed for that. But when a vain man puts on the garment of humility, the danger is that he will take to admiring the garment. That he fall not into this danger — become proud of his humility — let the youth now keep very near the Heavenly Powers. In them alone lies his safety.

The Heavenly Powers do not intrude on the soul of man. Even when working with him they keep their hands off him; even when saving him they preserve in him the consciousness that he is working out his own salvation. Hence the Sons of Aklis can deliver Shibli Bagarag in no other way than by subjecting him to a process of moral and spiritual discipline. Let it not be thought that the method of their discipline — making the youth, as crowned King of Apes, bear the sickening burden of his crown — is out of place here. Like all regions of the Allegory, this exalted region is none other than the real world; its exaltation consisting in its being the real world as seen by the spiritual man, and as furthering by its disciplines the purification of spirit. It is not always fine experiences that minister to refinement. To acquire a cleansing disgust at filth man may sometimes require to have his nose rubbed in it. The Heavenly Powers are not dainty in their methods of discipline, would not need to be when it is man they are disciplining. It is no incongruity then that though in their presence and under their tuition, Shibli Bagarag should have sickening experiences with that ignoble rabble. the crowd of men-apes. Through such experience his cleansing is to come.

As mere satire, however biting, no objection need be taken to the representation of human beings as a rabble of apes, their affairs comparable for unimportance to the meaningless squabbles of apes. But in this connection it is not mere satire. It is designed to indicate Shibli Bagarag's attitude towards his fellow men, the attitude approved of by the Heavenly Powers. None the less it must be pronounced a wrong attitude. Contempt is a lesson taught not in God's school but in Satan's. To despise your fellow-men is to prove yourself their inferior. It is not engaging in petty affairs that makes you petty. It is standing superciliously aloof from such affairs, or, if engaging in them, engaging in a petty spirit, that makes you petty. Still in the Allegory matters could not properly have been represented otherwise. The representation is justified by its dramatic truthfulness, its psychological inevitability. Feelings which are strong enough to have cleansing power are never altogether well balanced. Man is in dominion to extremes, works out his salvation by means of extremes. As reaction from his former excessive delight in the buzzings and flatteries of men it is natural, for the moment right, that Shibli Bagarag should experience loathing. As to the naturalness of it there can be no question, for no relationship that can exist between men is so prolific in the seeds of ultimate contempt as the relationship of flattery. Even in regard to the honest applause of one's fellows, while it is good in the mass and at a distance, yet somehow to come close to it, reap it in detail, is ever to a noble spirit ignominy and weariness. This is Shibli Bagarag's experience. As popular favourite, crowned King of Apes, he is made to feel the burden of his crown. At all sorts of gatherings his presence, and on all sorts of matters his opinion, is in request. Once he rejoiced in this popularity, counted it greatness, but now that his ambition is rekindled, that he has risen from his benumbing throne, he counts it weariness, sickening waste of time. Also he perceives, since coming to close quarters with them, the worthlessness of his flatterers. They praise him, but do n't appreciate him; hail him as great, and would yet drag him down, have him prostitute his talents to the nothings of the hour. Pah! they are apes, not men; his gorge rises at them. These thoughts and feelings, nothing else, are what are symbolised by the Gall of the Roc, through touch of which deliverance comes. The Gall is the bitterness of sin, more accurately perhaps, in Shibli Bagarag's case, the disgust at sin. According to the Allegory, when *tasted*, as by the men-apes, the Gall works evil; when merely *touched*, as by Shibli Bagarag, it works good. The distinction is important. It is good to know that "the wages of sin is death," but the knowledge, if too thorough, itself means death. Man may sin himself out of the sweets of sin, but never out of the love of sin. To drink the cup of pleasure to the dregs, so tasting its sedimentary bitterness is a sure way to bring about not repentance but pessimism in its most unholy form. Creatures whom Satan has thus sucked dry,

become eager impotences, nests of unholy memories. Cynicism, chief among
the secondary symptoms of this unwor-
thiest pessimism, settles on them. They
become keen but unclean critics of
life, bubbling over with Byronic bitterness. But poisons when rightly applied
have generally medicinal virtues. A
taste of the Gall of the Roc kills; a
touch of it may make alive. Notice,
for it is very important, that in Shibli
Bagarag's case disgust at sin was the
result rather than the inspirer of repentance. The inward reaction had commenced, he had set himself against the
love of, before he acquired the distaste
for flatteries. It was not the Gall which
brought repentance; it was repentance
which brought the Gall. This indeed
is how most accurately to distinguish
between the touch and the taste of the
Gall. When man by repentance invites the Gall to come, it merely
touches him to the cleansing of his
soul. But when it comes without invi-
tation, forces itself — as always soon or
late it does — on the unwilling and un-
repentant sinner, the sinner is made
taste it, and the taste is death. It was
168

therefore because Shibli Bagarag welcomed the Gall, commissioned the men-apes to bring it to him, that at its touch the ass-eared crown fell from his head. He thus obtains deliverance from his besetting sin of vanity, first *intellectually* by self-criticism — symbolised by his liberating laughter on the throne ; second *spiritually* by rooting the love of flattery from his heart — symbolised by the touch of the Gall. Otherwise put, his will rises in arms against his vanity, and, for such is the operation of of grace, the heart follows the will, to the rooting out of vanity.

The feastings and festivities of Shibli Bagarag with the Sons of Aklis, in particular that feasting under the branches of the miraculous fruit tree, clearly symbolise the spiritual nourishments and refreshments which came from his communion, wrestling, with the Heavenly Powers. Here Shibli Bagarag is lifted above objective experience. God touches him, not through the medium of such experience, but directly, spirit with spirit. Man's noblest prerogative is this power to withdraw himself from the world, to enter as free spirit into the

169

L

presence chamber of the Father Spirit. It is thus he becomes equipped for high enterprise. The human spirit is nourished, kept in strength and cheer, by the Divine. But while all are made free of the common bounty, a special table, stored with royal nutriment, is reserved for the seekers, the wrestlers, who as princes prevail with God. Shibli Bagarag is of the number. He sits under the branches of the miraculous fruit tree, eating the fruit thereof.

By these disciplines and nourishments it is that he is fortified for the demand now to be made on him, even that renunciation which is the price of the Sword. His surrender of the Spells to Gulrevez, as symbolising the consummation of his long training, is of special importance. Notice these points with respect to Gulrevez. *First* — In her form of Antelope it was no easy task catching her. Much pursuit was required, "a hawk being let loose to worry and distress her timid, beaming eyes." *Second* — She was the one, alone permitted, to hold speech with Aklis, the Father, behind the Veil. *Third* — After Shibli Bagarag had surrendered

the Spells to her she resumed her
proper shape, which was that of a
damsel "a vision of loveliness with
queenly brows." Truth will gleam from
these statements if we take Gulrevez
to represent that spirit of self-renunciation to which, to be a chosen soldier
of the Lord, Shibli Bagarag had now to
attain. That is a spirit which comes to
no man naturally and without effort.
It must, like Gulrevez, be hunted after,
captured at the cost of struggle and
pain. And it is the condition of soul
necessary for communion with God.
When man truly prays, it is the Gulrevez in him that prays. None but she
can go behind the Veil to speak to
Aklis. And as for the change of form
which she took after the surrender of
the Spells, is it not happily true that
every act of self-denial appears beautiful in retrospect? The resolution to
perform such an act eludes us, flies
before us like an Antelope. We must
use violence, worry and distress ourselves, to come by it. But once the
surrender has been made, our soul is
aglow with the sweetness and beauty
of it. The Antelope becomes a damsel

"a vision of loveliness with queenly brows."

Only one of the three hairs from the tail of the horse Garraveen was Shibli Bagarag called on to surrender to Gulrevez. Which enthusiasm did that lost hair represent? Not surely the Muskball enthusiasm, for the natural joy man has in his work is entirely compatible with the spirit of self-surrender. Genius is not robbed of itself when given up to the service of God. Still less could it have been the Sign of the Crescent enthusiasm, for that as being a drudge's enthusiasm is not only compatible with but the inevitable concomitant of self-surrender. Gulrevez would not deprive Shibli Bagarag of that mighty Hair, rather she would touch it with her divine fingers as it circled the wrist of the youth, increasing so its potency, endowing it with gleams of livelier light. The Call of Battle enthusiasm, "the sapphire hair that conquered the lion" was what Shibli Bagarag had to part with. It could have been no other, need not even have been this but that he was "tempted by the third temptation in Aklis, and left not the

PURGATION

Hall in triumph, the Hall of the Duping Brides." A man may conceivably be a selfless man, entirely surrendered to God, though in action he manifests that heat of blood, *gaudium certaminis*, which the Call of Battle enthusiasm is. But to a man of Shibli Bagarag's temperament the thing was impossible. The battle fervour would be certain to stir up self-love, set flame to vanity in his heart. Therefore to become a selfless man his selfhood had not only to be surrendered, it had to be emasculated. His weakness was so entwined round his strength that in pulling up the one the other had to suffer damage. To human nature in its progress toward the divine it must often happen so. Men under discipline of the spirit cannot always front the world with that appearance of strength which belongs to those who live full-based on their natural instincts. They are in the remaking and exhibit some of that instability inevitable to the process. Surely Shibli Bagarag's discipline under the Heavenly Powers was a terrible one when it led to the uprooting, casting from him, one of the most deeply seated instincts of his nature.

Surrender is the last word God has to say to man. All spiritual training in its beginning is a seeking, in its completion a surrendering. God beggars us to enrich us. He takes our all that in return He may give us His all. There would have been something conspicuously lacking in the Allegory, we would have missed in it the secret of Christ, had Shibli Bagarag's strenuous seeking not been made to end in surrender. Is it not partly at least patent to reason that surrender is the necessary condition of strength ? A man cannot do great things from small motives. He cannot Master an Event for the personal glory of the achievement. If he thinks to fight God's battle to advertise his own prowess, it is not God's battle he is fighting, for "Allah's the cause with no fleck of self stained." Masters of Events, saviours of the world, have necessarily escaped from cramping and betraying personal motives. They are men who resolutely sacrifice themselves, and who hold the Sword at the price of sacrifice. By

PURGATION

finally abandoned self - seeking, by
sinking himself and all that he had
in his cause, Shibli Bagarag became
a mighty and a consecrated power.
The Sword of the Lord was in his
hands.

EQUIPMENT

THE Sword, the emblem of the power by which Shibli Bagarag is to accomplish his Reformation, bears two meanings. These meanings, as being alike legitimate, would be found, on full analysis, to largely resolve themselves into each other. Still they are sufficiently distinct to call for separate notice.

Two factors, the personal and the impersonal, go to the making of every achievement. The Master of the Event and the Spirit of the Age alike contribute a share. No man, however qualified by spells, can be a reformer unless he finds ready to his hands social forces which make for reform. Had Luther been born a century earlier he could never have succeeded in breaking the power of Rome — the Sword for the Mastery of that Event not having then been sharpened. The Sword may be

177

taken to represent the impersonal factor in man's work, that which he gets given him by his time. The Sons of Aklis, sharpeners of the Sword, would thus personify the Time-Spirit, the sum total of those forces which are ever at work in society ripening things for change. Yet since God achieves his purpose through the Time-Spirit, the Sons of Aklis cease not, even in this connection to be the Heavenly Powers — personifications of the Providence of God in relation to men. The Allegory is entirely catholic. The reformer needs to have given him his weapons; so does the scientist, the artist, the worker of every kind. Suitable materials and conditions must be supplied by the Time-Spirit; otherwise, no matter for his spells, man can accomplish but little.

The Sword, the emblem of destruction, is especially apt as a description of the reformer's tools. His work is to build up indeed, but it is firstly and chiefly to cut down. Something else would doubtless have to be substituted for Shagpatism, but meantime the matter in hand was destruction. The world is saved by change. A noble inconsistency runs through the ages. Men serve God to-day by building; they serve him to-morrow by demolishing what is built. Nature is ever at war. Her peace is but the antagonising of equal forces. Her stillness is but the stillness of sense-baffling motion. The world is saved by change, and Shagpat's hour has come. He has outlived his usefulness; is now indeed a mere corruption, a dead thing and the spreader of death. Expeditious burial is what he requires; but the world's Shagpats can never have expeditious burial owing to the vested interest certain people have in their corpse. Shagpat cannot even be granted a death-certificate; the Lords of Vested Interest—honourable hoaxers all—swearing on soul and conscience that he is still alive, serving his day and generation nobly as ever. But God gets weary of lies. This dead thing — fronting the living, feigning the wholesome offices of life — has to be removed. Perhaps had he consented in time to moderate reform, say to that friendly, conservative shave Shibli Bagarag once proposed for him, his day of grace might not yet be over. But Shagpat scorned the art of timely concession, no hair in all his head would Shagpat consent to part with. There he stands, fronting the light of day, an overgrown evil, a tangled wilderness of hairiness — untaught, unteachable, sublime in stupidity! His day of grace is past. No friendly, conservative shave for Shagpat now. It is the Sword of Aklis Shibli Bagarag carries.

Transcendental wisdom proclaims Pre-established Harmony, clockwork Providence, the moment bringing the man. But is there ever a time when God is not urgently advertising for a man to "rid the world of nuisances," constant employment and good wages — mainly in thwacks — being guaranteed? Suitable candidates may come too late, but not surely too soon. For were a Shibli Bagarag to present himself in Aklis, demanding the Sword before it was sharpened, he would simply be set to sharpen it — very honourable employment indeed. True, in that case he would not be the Master of an Event, but merely the forerunner; but some of the world's best men have been such. Peace notwithstanding to Pre-established Harmony and all transcendental wisdom. Destiny keeps trust with Shibli Bagarag in most honourable fashion. The Sword is ready, and into no hands but his can it be given. Every great movement tends to focus itself in, and to accomplish itself through one individual. The history of the world is the history of its great men. Fate indeed uses the many to put might and keenness into the blade, but when it is fit for service she entrusts it into the hands of one.

This last thought suggests the other meaning of the Sword. Though coming second in point of exposition, it must be considered the primary meaning, the one Meredith had mainly though not exclusively in view. I will state it briefly.

Where there is no reformer, ripeness for reform passes into rottenness, death itself thus becoming reformer. For though in the spirit of man there is inexhaustible recuperative power, it is a power which, speaking of men in the mass, seems incapable of awakening into spontaneous activity. Though the

world is never past mending, it is yet
never able to mend itself. A physician,
a reformer is required. God deals in
go-betweens. He speaks to one man,
and through that one man to the age.
The place of a leader — a true leader —
is thus supremely great. In regard only
to official Kingship is the Divine Right
of Kings an exploded doctrine. Of that
other Kingship which resides not in
office but in personality it is an eter-
nally true doctrine. Men of richly commanding personality breathe out upon
their age the greatness of their own
spirit. Their power is not something
they derive from, but something they
impart to, the world. In themselves,
the dæmonic resources of their own
nature, resides their power. Such men
— the world has had many of them —
are themselves to be called Swords. In
most cases Sword is the word which
literally describes them. Great epochs
of history are marked, made rather, by
the apparition of colossal men — storm-
centres, fountains of battle — whose
destiny for good or evil it is never to
enjoy peace, never while they live to
let the world enjoy it. Like living

EQUIPMENT

Swords they flash continual war, and truly their swords are miraculous weapons, drawn from the armoury of their own spirits. It is not only or chiefly of professional soldiers, men like Napoleon, that this is true, for indeed of quite another class of men it is far more profoundly true. Not they who deal in gunpowder, but they who deal in ideas are the real storm-centres of the world. Ideas alone are mighty; in them lie the dynamite to destroy and the power to recreate the things of men. Hence it was that the Prince of Peace could declare that he came "not to send peace but a sword." And truly a sword he did send. Napoleon's sword perished and sunk to quiet rest with himself, but the Sword of Christ is still at its mighty work, passing from hand to hand and from age to age, and no man can say unto it "Peace, be still." Not by the world, nor of the things of the world, are swords of this temper fashioned. "From worlds not quickened by the sun," even from that region where men commune with the Sons of Aklis, and make surrender to Gulrevez, do such swords come. God's Swords

are men, spirits breathed upon by His
Spirit. They come forth armed with
His inspirations, bringing with them
new ideas, new hopes, new outlooks
for men; imparting to them some
energy of life, outbreathing of creative
force, for the rebirth of the world.
This was the case with Shibli Bagarag.
His Sword was himself — what else
could it have been? Man is his own
treasure house. The Kingdom of God,
all resources of abiding wealth and
strength, are within him. He must become what he would get, so only can
he truly get. None the less blame not
man that his energies are mainly di-
rected outward, for it is so that, in
terms of his nature, he comes into possession of the inward. God traps man
into nobility, lets him like Saul go far
afield in search of asses, that in the
height of the search he may burst upon
him with the vision of a kingdom. All
earnest seekers are in the way of grace;
the idlers, the dilettanti only miss life's
lesson and life's blessing. But notice
again, for it is all important, how it was
that Shibli Bagarag became the Sword.
It was not purely in virtue of his Spells

184

— his splendid moral and intellectual qualities. These necessarily counted for much, gave him no small influence over his fellows. But something was required to convert Shibli Bagarag, the Spell-bearer into that immeasurably mightier being, Shibli Bagarag the Sword-bearer. It was renunciation. Renunciation wrought in him the divinest, mightiest of miracles. At touch of it the man arose transfigured, no longer merely a much-talented man, but a living Sword, of keenness to execute the purposes of the Lord. The world possesses no truer, mightier Allegory than this.

Everything in connection with the Sword and the getting thereof is significant, but I need refer only to these further points.

Shibli Bagarag had to face a mighty lion, thrust his hand into a fiery furnace, before he was permitted to grasp the Sword. The Sword itself was a thing of terror; its hilt "two large live serpents," venomous ones, promising death to him who grasped it. Also it was so large, "full a mile long," it seemed madness for man to attempt

M

to move it. Shibli Bagarag was thus involved in destructions and sheer impossibilities. He saw no way out of them, nor — and this is the point — did he ask to see any. He simply *dared*. Always he thought to go forward meant destruction, and always he "concealed his thought" and went forward. Always he thought the thing he had to do was impossible, and always he "concealed his thought" and did it. The teaching is excellent. No man will go far who puts his foot no further forward than he sees his way to draw it back. He must count on no drawing back, make no provision for drawing back, only so can he go truly forward. Certainly if he aspires to power — to wield the Sword of Aklis — he must dare and dare and evermore dare, for the moment he falters the Sword will fall from his grasp. This is not to be counted recklessness. Recklessness is that which is opposed to caution, but daring is that which is above caution. Daring is a great virtue, but only so when exercised on great matters; on other matters the virtue of caution is better. When, at the bidding of Gulrevez, man acts in disregard of consequences, it is daring; but at other bidding, it is recklessness. Hence we are told that when Shibli Bagarag feared to thrust his hand into the furnace at the command of the Sons of Aklis, it was Gulrevez who whispered in his ear "Do their bidding and be not backward. In Aklis fear is ruin and hesitation a destroyer."

As has been said the beauty of Gulrevez signifies the sweetness, the subtle delight which self-renunciation brings. To luxuriate in that sweetness, linger in self-gratulation over the thought of one's own nobility, is to gaze transfixed at the beauty of Gulrevez. This was Shibli Bagarag's condition, for which Gulrevez sharply rebuked him. "Hast thou nought for the Sword but to gaze before thee in silliness. . . . . . Shame on thee." Shibli Bagarag was here suffering under what Meredith in his "Farina" described as "the back-blows of Sathanas." To do a good deed and then admire yourself for doing it, an act of self-denial and then luxuriate in its sweets, is to be transfixed with the beauty of Gulrevez,

187

suffering so one of the deadliest "back-blows of Sathanas." It is thus that great deeds of virtue bring great danger to the soul. Satan reaps a fine harvest by following at the heels of men who commit noble actions, tripping them by their nobility. There are times when it is unlucky for a man to look at himself. As a bride avoids her mirror when robed in bridal attire, so ought man when robed in attire of hero; otherwise he will see and become enamoured of the Gulrevez within himself. This Allegory is to be compared with that of Goorelka offering Shibli Bagarag the dew of the Lily to drink.

After the Sword there was given Shibli Bagarag, as complementary equipment, the bird Koorookh. The signification of the bird is discovered by consideration of its origin. It came by the stirring of a fountain with the Sword. The fountain had but "the top spray of it touched with a beam of light and the air breathed of man," yet when Shibli Bagarag stirred it with the Sword "the whole body of it took a leap towards the light that was like the shoot of a long lane of silver in the moon's

188

rays, and lo, in its place the ruffled feathers of a bird." Take the fountain to represent Shibli Bagarag's heart, his inner self. The stirring of it with the Sword, its consequent "leap towards the light" would then simply mean that ferment, exaltation of spirit, which came of his new-born consciousness of power. No man on whom dawns the knowledge that he is a man apart, equipped for some great destiny, but must be profoundly affected, greatly elevated by the knowledge. His heart, stirred by the Sword, takes a "leap towards the light." No name that can be given to Koorookh altogether brings out its meaning, but if name of some sort is required, call it Faith. The service it rendered was to support Shibli Bagarag on its wings, and is not faith an exaltation, a winged support to the Spirit of man? Mounted on Koorookh the youth in the exuberance of his gladness waved the Sword, and lo "the sun lost that dullness on its disk and took a bright flame, and threw golden arrows everywhere; and the pastures were green, the streams clear, the sands sparkling." In the light of

his own joy everything smiled. It was
an experience that could not last, but
could never be effaced. The man has
had his revelation of life's radiant possibilities, and the memory of it will
live with him in his hours of gloom.
The bird Koorookh survives the exaltation of spirit in which it is born,
abides with the man, doing him service.

The Sons of Aklis, sharpeners of the
Sword, have at last done their work
with Shibli Bagarag. They were girding
him while as yet he knew them not.
His thwackings, his hungers and hardships were of them, so also his striv-
ings and strayings, victories and failures. By things outward and inward,
life's happenings and the siftings and
disciplines of spirit, they were working
on him, sharpening him. Sore has it
been on Shibli Bagarag, this sharpening; surely now he may have breathing
time to take joy in its results. 'T is
no base region, but an exalted and honourable region of Aklis he is in. In
the high fellowship of these the Sons
of Aklis, and in that of Gulrevez, the
Divine One, may he not linger blamelessly? And this Sword, gotten at so

great price, what glory, what delectation
of spirit it brings! Heaven and earth
laugh in the miracle of its light. Surely
he may bide a little in this honourable
region of Aklis, waving the Sword, so
making celestial holiday. But no, the
Sons of Aklis and Gulrevez forbid. "To
work with the Sword" is their stern, im-
patient command. As the candlestick
carries light not for its own good, but
for the good of the household, so is
it with Shibli Bagarag and his Sword.
If he holds it as a private possession
the two poisonous serpents which are
its hilt will fasten on his hand, biting it.

TEMPTATION

EVERY condition of soul carries in itself its own danger. Man is never so high that Satan cannot get at him to tempt him. Shibli Bagarag as bearer of the Sword endures two temptations; the first arising from an interplay between his strength and his weakness, the second arising from his strength only. The second is immeasurably the more dangerous. A man needs the consciousness of weakness to protect him from his own strength. He who knows himself to be at once weak and strong is merely on the eve of a temptation: he who knows himself wholly strong is on the eve of a fall. Consider first that temptation which came to Shibli Bagarag from interplay between his strength and weakness. It is represented in the Allegory by Noorna and her dangers as seen through the eye of Aklis.

Until he got the Sword the idea of
shaving Shagpat could remain only a
fixed but unrealisable idea in Shibli
Bagarag's mind. The pivot idea it was
round which consciously or uncon-
sciously his life moved, yet none the
less it lay shut up in himself, could
not be put into operation. That is
symbolised by Noorna imprisoned on
the Pillar, waiting for the liberating
Sword. This Pillar, as was formerly
explained, must be taken to represent
the will. Every scheme of ambition
which a man cherishes, but which,
through lack of power, he cannot meantime put into execution, is a Noorna
imprisoned in the Pillar waiting for the
liberating Sword. Too often Noorna
waits in vain, is left neglected to fall
a prey to Karaz, the fish. The ambition
which a man cannot directly work at,
he must at least work up to, otherwise
it will cease to be his ambition, fall
quite off the Pillar of his will into the
jaws of that Evil One who feeds on
deserted Noornas. With Shibli Bagarag
in this respect all is well. So strenuously has he worked up to his ambition that the Sword for its realisation

is now in his grasp. At last therefore the time has come for Noorna's liberation, for that long cherished idea of shaving Shagpat to be put into execution. *Noorna is actually running up the blade of the Sword to reach her betrothed,* a symbol — surely a suggestive one — of the fact that power to accomplish duty brings duty immediately, urgently before us. From that urgency comes Shibli Bagarag's temptation. In emerging from the abeyance life of the Pillar — the dormant recesses of the will — into the urgency of immediate duty — in running along the Sword to meet her betrothed — Noorna encounters much danger. Doubts, difficulties, tumults of thought arise in Shibli Bagarag. His strength and weakness are in conflict; but notice, for the point is in his favor, 'tis through his strength he has come to the knowledge of his weakness. Formerly, when he was quite unfit to shave Shagpat, the task seemed to him easy; but now in the light of the Sword which qualifies him for the shave he perceives it to be a task of appalling magnitude, beset with difficulties and dangers past computing.

His very fitness for the work is thus a mirror revealing to him his unfitness. Humility of this nature — the humility which is the concomitant of true strength — does indeed in some sort expose a man to danger. But 't is a saving danger; were Shibli Bagarag not exposed to it he would be exposed to worse. As to the precise nature of his experiences nothing need be said. The Kite, the White Ball, the Red Serpent — these, to be sure, might readily be given some more or less definite meaning by relating them to the powers which respectively overcame them. But it will be better — more in harmony with Meredith's design — to leave them in their suggestive indefiniteness. Note only that the powers which overcame them were Faith (Koorookh), Self-denial (Gulrevez), and Providence, perhaps here better called the Grace of God (the Sons of Aklis). Are not these, these alone, the powers by which man overcomes temptation? Could Meredith have described in more Christian fashion the helps that avail in spiritual warfare?

The temptation next to be considered,

that described in the Allegory of the Veiled Figure, was not an interplay between strength and weakness; it was strength unprotected by weakness, tempted so to run riot, overreach itself, and become itself weakness. One's difficulty in regard to this Allegory is not to discover but to speak on its meaning. Shibli Bagarag's experience was here an essentially ineffable one. Only as standing outside it, looking at it from the aloofness of intellectuality, is speech at all possible. Then indeed so magically rich is the Allegory, into such variety of intellectual settings can its truth be put, that the difficulty might be to put a limit on speech. I shall merely state the broad meaning of the Allegory.

A seer in his first flush of seership is apt to set eternity over against time to the dwarfing of time's affairs; afterwards when his seership is ripe he finds eternity in time to the enriching of time's affairs. Shibli Bagarag is new to the uses of seership. It is his conversion morn. He does not overvalue, cannot overvalue, the wonderful spiritual treasure that has come to him;

but in the light of it he grossly under-
values all else. The world and the
things of the world appear to him as
nothingness; meaning and value quite
knocked out of them. This is a danger
incident to profound spiritual experience. It is perhaps inevitable that a
man on his first awakening to the reality of spiritual things should be seized
with the conviction that the world and
its concerns are Rabesqurat, illusion.
The conviction carries danger in it. He
who thinks the affairs of time meaningless has necessarily a shallow outlook
into eternity. He who turns his back
on the world, scouting it as Rabesqurat,
is living in a spiritual vacuum, with the
devil of pride for company. The man
of mature and rightly developed spirituality flashes his Sword, not to peer
through, but to enrich and illumine the
Veil. Giving forth of his own reality
unto Rabesqurat he perceives her to
be, not an idle and delusive show, but
a mystery replete with the wisdom and
subservient to the purposes of God.
But spirituality, though the ultimate
unifier, begins in antagonisms. Shibli
Bagarag's great treasure does not en-

rich; it dwarfs, knocks meaning and value out of life. The Sword, given him to help the world, has revealed to him that the world is not worth helping. Had the Sword been first used to shave Shagpat, we may be sure it would have shed a kindlier, if not less piercing light on Rabesqurat; for he only can sanely criticise the world who is actively engaged in helping it. As it is, Shibli Bagarag brings his knowledge of spiritual values to bear, not helpfully, but antagonisingly on world-life — just the danger incident to his condition as one "born again."

What the Veiled Figure is no man knows; it seems fated that those who seek to know shall behold in it Rabesqurat. It is a discovery carrying penalty with it. A healthy life is after all one lived on the surface of things. This fair phenomenal world, this magic realm of appearances is not with impunity to be shattered by human thought. "Whom God deceives is well deceived." They who think not to let even God deceive them are made pay a penalty. In the case of philosophers, the penalty, let it be admitted, appears

trifling. It is possible for them to prove
that life is Maya, illusion, and after due
smack of self-gratulation at the clever-
ness of their proof, to return to life
and its concerns with undiminished
zest. But it is not by the fierce light
of the Sword philosophers peer at the
Veiled Figure; rather by the mild light
of academic thought, light oftimes with
the soot of vanity in it. No conclusion
so reached is likely to interfere with
digestion. But let us do them justice.
There have been philosophers who
took their own discovery badly, were
affected by it even unto pessimism.
As having peered behind the Veil,
and seen the nameless sight, these
sad initiates, wisdom-blighted ones,
took on them to become garrulous
preachers of despair. But surely of
all cants this cant of dilettante pessimism — outcome for the most part
of intellectual snobbishness — is the
worst. Men of action are seldom pessimists, yet properly speaking none
but men of action can be pessimists.
Only when a man peers at the Veiled
Figure by the flashing of the Sword
is he frozen into horror; peered at by,

other light he is but quickened into garrulity.

Shibli Bagarag is not a man of action diverted at a critical moment in his career to the exercises of philosophy; nor is he a Hamlet-like mortal industriously spinning a network of sophistries wherein to entangle his will. He is a seer blinded by his own seership. As man of action it was certainly binding on him to enquire into the value, the reality of such definite phenomena as from time to time he had to deal with. But this was not an enquiry into the reality of definite phenomena; it was an enquiry into the reality of phenomenal life altogether, a facing of the ultimate problem as to whether the Veiled Figure that ferried on the waters of time was not in its very essence Rabesqurat. Yet enquiry is not the right word to use here. The case with Shibli Bagarag merely was that in the light of his own spirituality, his passionate reality, he looked at the Veiled Figure, the Mystery of Life, and that there burst upon him — he could not himself well tell how — the ghastly revelation that all, good and

N

bad in it alike, was illusion. It was intuition, illumination, flash of the Sword of thought. No spiritual catastrophe could have been more complete. Coming as it did when he was on the eve of battle, body and soul of him braced for great enterprise, his whole strength suddenly toppled over and became weakness. His consuming earnestness landed him in indifference, his heroic struggle after reality in the squalid conviction that life was illusion. As by a stroke of evil magic the man, just when he seemed at his strongest, was suddenly converted into a limp, listless, altogether pitiable creature. Such abrupt and tragic reactions are not uncommon in life, and though they take widely different forms, they are all traceable to the same psychological principle. They come from peering through some Veil, discovery of some paralysing truth. The main-spring of the altruism of Timon of Athens was a subtle, but not ignoble, egoism. He believed his lavish gifts were but investments, money lodged in the Bank of Gratitude, for which, though he never thought to ask it, interest at any

time would be available. But when
on peering through the Veil of human
nature, he discovered he had been cher-
ishing an illusion, his love toppled over
on the other side, became snarling,
vitriolic hate. Love which expects
nothing would not be subject to such
reactions. It could pour itself forth and
suffer no check from the baseness of
its beneficiaries. But this, while it may
seem nobler, is really not so noble as
exacting love. In any case it was not,
could not in the nature of things have
been Shibli Bagarag's love. He had to
expect something from the world, could
not labour to help it unless as cherish-
ing such expectation. When a man in
setting about the work of patching an
old garment, discovers the garment to
be so rotten that it cannot hold the
thread, there is necessarily an end to
his patching. So with Shibli Bagarag
— he who thought to patch, reform the
world. Had he been a man to find
content in other-worldliness, he might
at this crisis have found unholy healing
for his sorrow. But it was to help this
world, not to personally equip himself
for the other he had sought the Sword;

no private comfort could he take in the thought of other-worldliness. In that respect Shibli Bagarag's nobility did not forsake him. The case with him is that he is in a state of spiritual disease in which there is no baseness. Lament his condition we may; seriously blame him for it we cannot. It is his strength, unprotected by weakness, that has proved his undoing. It is his seership, untutored by its limitations, that has made him blind. This experience also was appointed unto the much-disciplined man, but there is hope that it will pass. Dilettante despair fattens with the years, but real despair cannot live long. All the good influences of life are in conspiracy against it. The experience may prove to the ultimate enrichment of Shibli Bagarag's soul. He has often been tripped by his weakness before, but this tripping of him by his strength may teach him a more watchful humility, a deeper, sadder wisdom by far.

For a time he is not to be helped, but Abarak, his faithful companion, does what he can. Two hairs — emblems of twin strengths — are still on the hero's wrist, spared to him by Gulrevez. These Abarak loosened, and behold they took the form of Genii, "sons of brilliance," acknowledging themselves so as "slaves of the Sword." The meaning seems to be that Abarak sought to restore Shibli Bagarag by stirring up, making appeal to the strength he knew to be in him. The result was to some degree successful. The youth's genius flashed into activity, radiated strength and brilliance, but alas, it was all non-personal. The man was not in it. "Slaves of the Sword" indeed were the Genii, but the Master of the Sword was asleep, had no commands to give. In happier circumstances the Hairs would have been allowed to remain quietly on Shibli Bagarag's wrist until he had emerged from Aklis, the time for their transformation into Genii being when the Master commenced his campaign against Shagpat. But Abarak was fain to try the experiment of awakening the man by means of his own strength. The result was that he awoke the strength but not the man.

The way of resolute will — which was

the way of the Seventh Pillar — being
thus blocked, Shibli Bagarag had to be
let dreamily drift, make return to active
life by plunging down through falling
waters; and drowning would have been
his doom but that Noorna was there to
receive him. It was through the bird
Koorookh's inability to pronounce her
betrothed's name that Noorna made the
discovery that he had peered through
the Veil, and "bore now a name that
might be uttered by none." So far as this
mighty emblem has speakable meaning,
this seems to be its meaning. When
the consciousness of eternity flashes
across the unripe soul, it obliterates the
consciousness of personality. Man
loses grip of himself, knows himself as
but a drop lost in the ocean; his name,
the symbol of his selfhood, cannot be
uttered. This was Shibli Bagarag's
awful condition. By his vision of time
and the things of time in the overpow-
ering light of eternity, he lost healthy
grip of his own identity. His faith in
the reality of his own selfhood tottered.
The bird Koorookh could not utter his
name.

The sleep in the bosom of Noorna

which restored Shibli Bagarag to his
active self is a beautiful Allegory, but
so simple that it scarcely needs interpretation. His ambition which in the
past had woven itself into, made itself
his life, slowly re-awoke within him —
a reason-restoring, vivifying influence.
It was a dream, could not for a time
be more. The man's thoughts were
upheaved, broken loose, scattered into
eternity; they had slowly and uncon-
sciously to co-ordinate themselves a-
fresh, and 't was round Noorna, she
who had been the spring of all his
activity, that they co-ordinated, recovering health and sanity so. The healing
process happily completed itself, and
Shibli Bagarag was himself again. Yet
never quite the same; none who peer
through the Veil can ever again be the
same. Something had entered his life
that could not be banished, and something had passed from it that could not
return. Henceforth we see in him a great,
stern, resolute man, wise and unflinch-
ing in his ways; but gone were the buoy-
ancy, the light-heartedness, the sweet
and dewy grace of earlier days. He
carried in his heart a dowry of sadness.

THE BALDNESS OF SHAGPAT

PLOTTINGS

A MAN who fights for duty's sake, and with no lust of battle in him, may be the best of men, but scarcely the best of soldiers. The war-instinct — the Call of Battle enthusiasm — in however purified a form, may be merely the survival of man's brute heritage, yet nothing so far accruing to him from his other, nobler heritage can quite take its place. Duty — the spur of the will — is nobler, but not so ready, so spontaneous in its strength, as instinct — the spur of the blood. Hence however it be with Shibli Bagarag as a man, as a soldier he is seriously weakened by the loss of that third in the Trinity of Strengths, sacrificed to Gulrevez in purgation of his vanity. But for that loss Noorna declared "earth could have planted no obstacle" to her lover's stroke. Not that, as it is, the reformer conducts his campaign listlessly; his sense of duty is too strong for that. But there is a deliberation, an uninspired caution in his methods, which the war-enthusiasm, were it still his, might have worthily redeemed by flash of brilliance and open daring. In nothing does the inspiration of the moment count for more than in battle, and Shibli Bagarag's far-seeing and elaborate plottings seem to leave him too little open to such inspiration. Still his plottings, on their own level, are not unworthy of the much disciplined man. As is fitting they are conducted unostentatiously; he himself, now happily free from the itch for publicity, keeping in the background. Without cruelty yet also without mercy is he to his followers, considering only what service each man can render, appointing him to that service regardless of the tenderness of his skin. Shall he who himself has endured thwacks, is ready to endure them again, shrink from endangering the skin of others? By Allah, 't were a weakness unworthy of the Master. How to win the battle is Shibli Bagarag's first thought; after that, and only so far as consistent with that, how to spare the soldier.

The "Plot" calls for little interpretation. It is not such a plot as in its entirety ever was or could be put into operation, and to that extent it must be pronounced unconvincing. But Allegory would be falling below its own level did it attempt, even in practical matters, to embody the prosaically practical. Its realm is the realm of principles; its function to present fact in the form of truth, to unshell the fact and give us the kernel. While leaving untouched most of the details of the "Plot," I make such references as seem necessary.

It is by the ruthless exploitage of Baba Mustapha that the plot is worked out. Baba, both by his strength and weakness, is eminently adapted for the purpose. He is not a man of faith; but so colossal is his self-conceit it simulates, and that not badly, many of faith's functions. Were it possible that counterfeit strength could be converted, by mere quantitative magnificence, into genuine strength, Baba would indeed be a man to be reckoned with. But it is not possible; and the man's virtues are tawdry at best, and subject to sudden collapse. If his self-importance prompts him to undertake great tasks, his pettiness of spirit betrays him to failure in the midst of them. To stand conspicuous in the forefront of things, doing nothing in the noisiest possible manner; to pose and fuss and gabble in the belief that he is the centre of movements and the controller of men — that is Baba Mustapha. In further justice admit him to be a persuasive and prolific theorist, professor in all its branches of the science of reform. Into whatever country Baba enters there he proposes reform. He is for shaving everybody and everything, carries tackle for the purpose, and inventions, lathering preparations of his own, guaranteed infallible. It is this brilliant fool whom Shibli Bagarag, he who has learned to "study men," ruthlessly exploits. Clearly it is impossible for such a man as Baba to co-operate with the Master, enter intelligently yet subserviently into his plans. Hence since he scorns to become a servant, he suffers the indignity of being made a tool; is led, blindfolded by his own vanity, whithersoever the Master wills. He jumps at the proposal that he should shave Shagpat, become himself Master of the Event. When he fails, as to be sure he does, care is taken that the Shagpatians are fully informed of the matter. The result — and this was the object of the plot — is that they become vaingloriously convinced that Shagpat is inviolable as under the protection of the Unseen. And truly the power to which Shagpat owed protection was after its sort an unseen power, being none other than a Flea. As symbol the Flea must be pronounced perfect. It stands for life's petty worries, those little everyday annoyances which distract man's attention, hinder him in his work. They abound everywhere assail everybody — that sort of Flea; but the man of passionate earnestness is scarcely, if at all, conscious of their attentions. Bite they never so assiduously they cannot disturb him in his work. Baba Mustapha — the shallow, vanity-inspired one — is tortured by the Flea, cannot because of it come at Shagpat with his razor;

but Shibli Bagarag — the deep, resolute man — no complaint of Fleas does he make. Is not this as good a test as any of the greatness, the work-outcome of a man? If you let life's distractions, its innumerable petty worries, break in upon and defeat your industries — by that token know yourself among the weaklings, those from whom good work cannot come. Like Baba Mustapha, in such case, you will likely be a mighty gabbler about your work, your schemes and determinations, but like him also you will be defeated by a Flea. All but a few are so defeated. It is the power of the microscopically small that has ever to be feared. Great temptations may summon man to himself, call forth correspondingly great resistance; but small temptations, as being small, put man off his guard. When Satan acts as vetoist it is in the form of a Flea that he acts; not openly forbidding man to do good, but disturbing him, frittering away his time, eating into him with life's round of petty distractions. One has only to look back on his past, witness the failures with which his years are

strewn, to confess to the mighty, life-
consuming power of the Flea.

So vainglorious have the Shagpatians
become that they no longer think of de-
fending Shagpat against the attentions
of barbercraft, rather they challenge
barbercraft to do its worst. Baba
Mustapha is compelled, in presence of
King and people, to make fresh attempts on Shagpat's head. Again he
suffers defeat, but not this time by the
Flea. It is by a wonder, even the
Burning of the Identical, defeat now
comes. As first meaning of the Allegory
the Burning of the Identical is to be
taken as the symbol of the spiritual
terrors of Shagpatism. Shagpat does
not need the scimitars of the King's
guard to defend him. An emergency
has but to arrive to prove that his real
strength lies not in the secular arm,
but in his own spiritual terrors. At
opposition, touch of would-be reformer's razor, there has but to be a Burning
of the Shagpatian Identical — a wrathful
display of spiritual authority — and the
would-be reformer is hurled back
"sprawling and spuming and uttering
cries of horror." How often in the past

o

has the Burning of the Papal Identical
flared over Christendom, a portent, a
thing of terror, even as that magical
Hair on the head of Shagpat! To this
day indeed when the Papal Identical
burns, it is a might and a miracle on
earth, millions of hearts acknowledging
the terrors of it. All offices and author-
ities may exhibit this burning of the
Identical, for all in essence are spiritual.
All men also may exhibit it; and indeed
it is when that spiritual might and
mystery which is the essence of one's
manhood asserts itself, flares forth in
its majesty, that the Burning of the
Identical becomes veritable miracle,
manifestation of the power of the Unseen. It need not be in wrath that the
Identical burns. Its mightiest burnings
are the burnings of love, and these are
the burnings which endure and subdue.
From Christ on the Cross did there not
arise a holiest, fiercest flame — reveal-
ment of that immortal energy of Love
which was and is the Identical of all
Identicals, even the Divine? The world
is still burning in that flame, will burn
in it till all is purified. Understand
therefore that the burning of the

PLOTTINGS

Identical is simply a manifestation of essential selfhood. Under ordinary conditions, alike in the case of men and institutions, the essential selfhood is never quite revealed, often as not indeed it seems quite hidden. But some great occasion arises, and the man or institution stands discovered. For good or evil the light shines, the Identical burns, and you have your revelation. In Shagpat's case the Burning of the Identical is best to be compared to the Spiritual terrors of Rome before which many brave men have fallen back "sprawling and spuming and uttering cries of horror."

The success of Shibli Bagarag's plot is marked by the temper of the Shagpatians. Behold the madness to which they have reached! They want to prolong a miracle, turn a miracle into a show. They want to put God's grace — for such they think it — on exhibition, keep it in operation for sensational purposes. This Baba Mustapha is a renowned barber, is he? None on earth more skilful in the science of barbercraft? Then he's just the man for us. Compel him to make another and yet another attempt on Shagpat. That will keep the miracle going; an excellent thing for the establishment of the faith; an excellent thing also — but that is by the way — for the prosperity of our city, and of us its worthy citizens. Was it not insanity? To invite danger in order to give divine grace its opportunity is to tempt God, and to tempt God is to court sorrow. Faith protects from evil, but when faith degenerates into presumption it is itself a great evil. God may take your part, but never in the spirit of a partisan. He is on your side so long only as you are on his side. If in a great emergency a great mercy has been vouchsafed you, do not provoke a similar emergency in the expectation of receiving a return of the mercy, for God will not be traded on. Shibli Bagarag's plottings have been terribly successful.

Was he justified in pursuing such plots, practising on his enemies in this fashion? This is really to ask whether war itself is justified, for war is essentially a game of wits rather than of gunpowder. But Shibli Bagarag was not at war in any other than the sense

that Luther was at war. His enemies
were his friends. It does not matter.
The prophet can afford to be candid,
but the practical reformer can seldom
afford to be altogether so. How far
and in what sense he may "employ
deceits" and yet keep his honour un-
tarnished is a large question, unnecessary to be discussed here. But was not
Shibli Bagarag by his deceits working
injury to the souls of these Shagpatians, basing his victory on their moral
deterioration, their spiritual insanity —
and do the ethics even of war justify
that? The ethics of war certainly do
not justify that. The general who
debases his enemy in order to prepare
defeat for them, is waging war on
humanity itself. Shibli Bagarag would
be defeating his own friendly purposes
towards the Shagpatians were he guilty
of this detestable thing. The case with
him however merely is that he pro-
vokes his opponents to feed fat on
their own folly, in the hope that the
after effects of the feast may wean them
from their folly. He encourages their
infatuation, lets their disease come to
a head in order the more speedily and

effectively to cure it. It is often 'the only way both with physical and spiritual troubles; and Shibli Bagarag's plot, his "deceits" when fully enquired into are seen to have meant nothing worse than this. All the same it must be admitted that one's moral instincts revolt against the employment of even such deceits for such purposes, and that to educate one's instincts into the required liberalism would be to run the risk of tampering with and weakening them. But it is by grappling with such problems, working them out, not with tortuous casuistry but in the light of that law of laws, which is the law of love, that man attains unto spiritual freedom.

BATTLES

IT has been previously mentioned, as a guiding principle of Meredith's work, that events in it are arranged not according to their time-relations, but according to their thought-relations. That principle must be borne in mind in our study of Shibli Bagarag's great fight with Shagpat. In the Allegory the fight is represented as coming at the end, forming the dramatic conclusion, the crowded climax of the reformer's career. As matter of fact since the hour of his betrothal to Noorna, he was always in some manner fighting Shagpat. This chapter therefore really represents not a part of his career, but his entire career viewed in its battle aspect. He did not delay his fight till he had gained the Sword; for indeed he gained, could only gain the Sword by and in the fight. At first a small weapon, it grew and increased mightily in his hands, till men knew it to be the veritable Sword of Aklis. Be it understood then that just as the Quest of the Spells represents Shibli Bagarag's career in its disciplinary, wisdom-seeking aspect, so the battle — the Flashes of the Blade — represents his career in its aggressive, Shagpat-reforming aspect; and that with him, as with Luther, these two ran side by side.

The account of the fight is altogether allegorical; and for point, rapidity, condensation, it is wonderful Allegory. Every detail here carries meaning, but to some of the more important only will it be necessary to refer.

Three times the blade flashed harmless, seemingly harmless lightning; at the fourth only was Shagpat's head touched, partly shaved. These flashes were not empty displays, purposeless preliminary flourishes that might have been dispensed with. In every Reformation the blade must flash before it strikes. How often before it struck did Luther's Sword flash what seemed harmless lightning over Papacy. Shagpat slept soundly, undisturbed by the flashing; he on whose head at that time rested Rome's Magical Hair slept also, but not quite so soundly. 'T is recorded that he muttered in his sleep, as if troubled by a pestilent dream, complaining of a "squabble among monks." " Coming events cast their shadows before." If it is the unexpected that happens, it is because we are unskilful readers of signs, for always in world-movements the Sword flashes before it strikes. In the French Revolution did not the mighty Sword then at work flash and flash before it struck to the destruction, the sweeping away of things that were? King and nobles knew not till too late what the flashing portended, and so their doom came on them.

But always besides the Flashes of the Blade there is darkness preceding great events. The darkness, be it noted, spake saying "I am Abarak of the bar, preceder of the Event." In all his relations Abarak represents will-power; here, as I think, it is not individual will-power, but the will of the people he must be taken to represent. The will of the people constitutes the riddle of destiny, the darkness into which those who would forecast events must struggle to peer. On the eve of great events the thundercloud, the portentous darkness which Abarak is, speaks; but few can interpret the voice beyond knowing that there is threat in it, prediction of the coming of some new, maybe monstrous thing. Hence men confront the future with wild forebodings, their "hearts failing them for fear, and for looking after those things that are coming on the earth." The universal panic of the hour, its uncertainties and alarms, are symbolised hyperbolically in the Allegory by fierce animals, creatures of the desert, crowding from all quarters into the city, tamed by terror. It is a feature preceding every great crisis in history, every "end of an age" this terror, foreboding, darkness; and always it is Abarak, the will of the people, which is the darkness. Could a nation see into that darkness it would behold its destiny.

Noorna also appears before the King, pleading for the life of Abarak and Feshnavat. "Delay the stroke yet

awhile O head of the magnanimous.
I am she claimed of Shagpat; surely I
am bride of him that is Master of the
Event, and the hour of bridals is the
hour of clemency." Noorna — the idea
of shaving Shagpat — surely the King
and all men were familiar with her,
knew of her betrothal with Shibli
Bagarag. But hitherto none permitted
themselves to believe that betrothal
would end in marriage. The idea of
shaving Shagpat, they fain thought,
would remain an idea, nothing more,
to the world's end. Now the signs of
the times — the flashes and the darkness
— put them in doubt. The betrothal
may after all be destined to be con-
summated; nay judging by these rapidly accumulating omens the hour
which is to see the shaving of Shagpat
is about to strike. Things being so it
occurs, is suggested to the King that
it might be wise to spare Feshnavat
and Abarak, for why, if the Star ·of
Shibli Bagarag is in the ascendant,
provoke him by the death of his
friends? "The hour of bridals is the
hour of clemency." But the King
hardens his heart. Even at this late

hour he thinks to stave off the threatened danger by energetic severity. Feshnavat, Abarak, all enemies of Shagpat must die. So may Shagpat yet triumph. Since this is the King's policy Shibli Bagarag must meet it, and that immediately, by policy equally energetic. The time for negotiation is past. The Sword flashes, not this time harmless lightning, but to the striking, shaving one side of Shagpat's head.

"As the moon sits on the midnight" so sits Shibli Bagarag on Koorookh, and the bird's vast wings "overshadow the entire land." It is a symbolical description of the man who, through possession of large assurance, strong-winged ambition, dominates his age. Master-spirits, great men of action may differ in other qualities, but one and all they sit on Koorookh, achieving so their tasks. And it is "as the moon sits on the midnight" that they sit; a regal light in the darkness, ruling and illumining the darkness. The grandeur, the poetic truth and beauty of the emblem must be manifest. The world contains no finer picture of those great men, master-spirits who come to the front in dark and troubled times, and to whom men turn for guidance as instinctively as they turn to the moon in midnight.

Notice that Shibli Bagarag's success was like to prove his undoing. The blood of his enemies, when he cleaved them with the Sword, proved fire, flowing "over the feathers of Koorookh, lighting him in a conflagration." Success, especially if come by early and easily, is like to be the forerunner of folly and failure. It sets Koorookh on fire; makes man's faith in himself and his star excessive; gives rise to that "vaulting ambition which o'erleaps itself, and falls on the other side." Shibli Bagarag escaped this danger. Koorookh, when in conflagration "flew constantly to a fountain of earth below, and extinguished it." To name the fountain with a name covering all its meaning would be difficult, and is unnecessary. It represents that saving consciousness of the limitations of man and the uncertainties of fortune which moderates one's confidence in his destiny, keeps him on the lines of sanity. It is the water of humility; and in it the bird Faith, after every victory, must bathe, lest it be consumed by the fires of presumption. For lack of this bathing it was that Napoleon perished. His Koorookh, plentifully drenched in the blood of his enemies, went thereby on fire, a very conflagration of presumption. His faith in his star became a magnificent madness, urging him to attempt, enabling him for a time seemingly to achieve the impossible. But in the end it betrayed him and laid him low. Had his Koorookh, when on fire, but stooped for cooling to the "fountain of earth below," surely Napoleon's fate would have been different. But if "nothing succeeds like success," nothing also may fail like success. Failure indeed is inevitable unless humility increases in proportion as victories accumulate.

Queen Rabesqurat proved Shibli Bagarag's most dangerous enemy in battle. "The terrible Queen streamed in the sky like a red disastrous comet . . . . and lo, there were suddenly a thousand Shagpats multiplied about, and the hand of Shibli Bagarag became exhausted with hewing at them." In

all political warfare, battles of reform,
misrepresentation plays a mighty part.
It matters not that the reformer has
studied deep into the social question,
laid his finger unerringly on the root-
grievance, the dominant injustice of
the day; in actual warfare it can hardly
be but that time and again he will suffer
confusion, make war on shadows. As
dominating his age the reformer is
necessarily more than most men sensitive to its influence; indeed he is the
common receptacle wherein its innumerable wisdom-mongers aspire to
deposit their wisdom. The inherent
perplexities of the problem are aggra-
vated for him by this babeldom of conflicting counsel. All sections of society
admit that something is grievously
wrong, that some Shagpat, monstrous
in hairiness, is blighting the world;
but as to what this Shagpat really is
scarcely any two sections are in agreement. The reformer is pelted with
conflicting opinions, not all of them
honest and disinterested. For real
Shagpatians, perceiving that he is
already working on dangerously right
lines, deliberately invoke the aid of

Rabesqurat, the "lying spirit," in order to lead him astray. Falsehoods, misrepresentations, illusive Shagpats, are multiplied by the thousand. The reformer's energies are exhausted with hewing at lies — surely the most wearisome, discouraging, disgusting part of his work. But it is work he cannot escape, for when Satan's kingdom is attacked Queen Rabesqurat, his best ally, never fails to "stream in the sky like a red disastrous comet."

Notable is the help little man Abarak renders Shibli Bagarag in this battle against lies. He threw a pellet on the eye of Aklis "and this sent out a stretching finger of beams and singled forth very Shagpat from the myriad of resemblances." It is unnecessary to consider whether it was in his individual capacity, or as spokesman, representative of the popular will that Abarak rendered this aid, for in truth it was in both capacities. There are occasions when the dunce can help the genius, help him better indeed than could a brother genius. Abarak's downrightness of purpose, his limitations in point of intellect, saved him from many of the confusions, the cross currents of thought, which perplexed Shibli Bagarag. It was not advice; it was a palpable something — a pellet, a fact, which the little man threw at the perplexed reformer. That, better than any subtlest argument, dispelled the reformer's fantasies, clarified his vision, gave him grip of realities again. As Baalam, in the matter of spiritual vision, his strong point, was surpassed and put to shame by his ass, so did it happen here. Shibli Bagarag's strength was to see facts, make facts *speak*, yet in this point of strength Abarak, the dull one, the aforetime slave of Rabesqurat, puts him to shame. It often happens so in life. The lessons taught a man by his inferiors are lessons which, if he learns at all, he learns thoroughly. Experience does not remove the boundaries and distinctions set up by thought, but it sometimes pitches us unceremoniously over them. There is doubtless a vast difference between the dunce and the genius, yet know them better and you may frequently have occasion to wonder which is dunce and which genius.

P

Notice the trick Shibli Bagarag played on Rabesqurat. He "put the blade between the first and second thought in the head of Rabesqurat, so that the sense of the combat became immediately confused in her mind, and she used her power as the fool does, equally against all, for the sake of mischief only." The meaning seems to be that Shibli Bagarag turned the tables on his enemies, confused by the subtlety of his tactics their sense of the position of affairs, as they had for a time confused his. Even had there been no subtlety on his part this was what was likely to happen. Queen Rabesqurat seldom remains long mistress of her own illusions. Whatever effect they may have on others, it is certain that his own lies confuse the liar. In every prolonged battle fought out largely with the artillery of falsehood, the combatants end by unwittingly turning their artillery against themselves. Lies may keep their ranks and mind their drill for a time, but sooner or later they get out of hand, prove anarchic soldiers, spreading confusion in both camps. Men will cease shooting if in doubt whether it is friend or foe they are shooting at, but in similar circumstances they will not cease lying. On the contrary it is then they will lie most industriously. Queen Rabesqurat was no longer mistress of her own illusions, but she did not on that account cease to produce illusions. While her head was clear she lied cautiously; when it became confused she lied at random, prolifically. When she thus uses her powers "as the fool does, equally against all," by that token know that the truth is about to prevail.

When Noorna saw how sorely Shibli Bagarag was put to it in the fight, she cried: "Yea though I lose my beauty and the love of my betrothed, I must join in this or he'll be lost." This daring Allegory deals with a great matter, and forms a fitting climax to the whole work. Shibli Bagarag's path to victory has all along been paved with sacrifice. Every bit of strength that is in him is the strength that comes of sacrifice. By a great self-surrender it was that he gained the Sword, and now nothing but a perilously greater surrender can make the Sword effective.

235

Noorna must enter the fight and take the risk. To understand what this means it is necessary to remember that Noorna has grown immensely since our first meeting with her. Merely as a living idea, engaging Shibli Bagarag's thoughts, she must have grown; but as a duty, engaging not his thoughts only but his activities, the growth has been great and of happiest quality. It is not reading into her an overstretch of meaning to say that she now represents, in the widest sense, Shibli Bagarag's holy of holies, that in him which is and which he would fain keep wholly pure. When the point of pride with a man has to do with his character, it is generally Pharisaism, moral faddism, bringing him some good maybe, but certainly much evil. But when it has to do with his work, the struggle to rightly accomplish his work, it is a seed of genuine nobility, having in it the potency of happiest growth. If a man is proud of his Noorna, strives to keep her clean and beautiful, she in return may make him, the whole of him, clean and beautiful. So is it with Shibli Bagarag. He owes his nobility to Noorna.

BATTLES

All of it is inspired by and centres
round her. Were she to cease to be his
dearest, worthiest pride, what pride,
what support would remain? It be-
hoves him therefore as he values his
soul's health to keep Noorna out of
risks. Behold her on the contrary in
the midst of risks, exposed in battle to
the venom of that scorpion whose sting
is fatal to beauty. It would be giving
the Allegory a too facile interpretation
to say that it merely means that in
their practical working out a man's
ideals must lose their virginal brightness, take on some stain of compromise. Neither would it be enough
to say that in the stress of battle — the
entanglements and compulsions of
practical affairs — a man inevitably falls
somewhat away from his own purity,
stumbles into actions of which his
conscience, in calmer moments, cannot
approve. The Allegory means that, but
surely it means vastly more. It shadows
forth a last and noblest sacrifice made
by Shibli Bagarag for his cause. If in
the nature of things the sacrifice was
not altogether deliberate — the thing
sacrificed being in a sense deliberation

itself — it only shows at what price of perilous nobility victory was purchased. If a man keeps thinking of himself, puritanically watchful of his soul's health, preferring rather to lose his cause than that his soul should suffer stain in the winning of it, then he is not yet ripe for victory. He must throw himself with selfless abandonment into the fight, holding nothing back, keeping nothing in reserve. Noorna even, his soul's treasure must enter the battle, and take the risk. This was the case with Shibli Bagarag, and in regard to it let no question of casuistry be raised; for in truth the man was on a plane of thought nobly removed from, exalted above casuistry. It was not a case of debating within himself whether or how far he would be justified in doing evil that good might come; it was a case of abandonment, disregardfulness of self, willingness, if necessary, to imperil his own soul in order to achieve his great purpose. "I could wish," said St. Paul, "that I myself were accursed from Christ for my brethren's sake"; and a similar ultra heroic spirit on the part of Shibli Bagarag is what is signified by Noorna entering the battle, risking the scorpion's sting to help her betrothed.

But behold the sequel to this great abandonment. No pleasure could Shibli Bagarag take in victory, when it came to him, because that Noorna "was withering from a sting of the scorpion shot against her bosom." The sting of the scorpion, the poisoned memory blighting that in him which was holiest and sweetest — what matter though he had come by it through utter surrender to his cause? He need not have come by it. Had he been resting aright on his strength his soul would have been safe, never safer than in abandonment; Noorna could have entered the fight and yet escaped the scorpion. If Shibli Bagarag has done wrong, why should he not suffer the consequence of his wrongdoing? Even the sins man falls into for God's sake, God will punish; even the sting Noorna comes by in the work of self-denial withers her beauty. Shibli Bagarag's peace of mind is gone. Success is poisoned for him by the sting of the scorpion. But if love washes away the sins committed against herself, much more will she wash away those men stumble into for her sake. Noorna is conveyed for nursing and healing to Gulrevez in Aklis — Gulrevez that was "alone capable of restoring her and counteracting the malice of the scorpion by the hand of purity." Thus ministered to, Noorna in due time returns to Shibli Bagarag "fair and fresh in the revival of health and beauty." Sins prompted by genuine love are but erring virtues; He who is Infinite Love will correct them in mercy, purge them from the venom of the scorpion, and receive them in beauty unto Himself.

SPOILS

CONGRATULATIONS to Shibli Bagarag! The degree of Master of an Event, highest and most-to-be coveted of degrees, has at last been conferred on him. The candidate for greatness has become great, God and man acknowledging his greatness. No sham crown prematurely snatched by the hand of vanity, but a real crown is what he wears now. May he not therefore at last settle down to restfulness and the blameless enjoyment of things? Holiday rest and enjoyment certainly, but nothing further; never again must he debase his head with that discarded fool's crown "the crown of him who hath achieved his ambition and resteth here." But surely if his life-work is accomplished there ought to be some sort of honourable superannuation for Shibli Bagarag. Impossible. There is no superannuation

241

for the man who loves his fellows.
Not even if he is a spent force, worn
out with much toiling? Impossible
again. The man who loves his fellows
is never a spent force. Love does not
fade with fading bodily powers, and
love is mightiest of forces. It is said
of the Apostle John that in his last
enfeebled days he was wont to have
himself carried to Church in a litter,
that from it, as from the most revered
of pulpits, he might whisperingly preach
to the people. Such as John could
never be a spent force. But if God never
superannuates his servants, never gives
them privilege of honourable idleness
in return for work done, what is
Shibli Bagarag's reward? Much every
way. For one thing, though a small,
there is the gratitude of his fellows.
To live on the gratitude of the public
is indeed next to living on its alms;
but this, Shibli Bagarag, the erstwhile
ass-eared one, is watchfully aware of.
No longer does he stay himself on
public favour, reckon it among his
abiding assets. But as having learned
to seek the approval of God, he is in
a position properly to estimate, and

therefore blamelessly to enjoy the approval of men. Also in the treasures of memory he finds genuine reward of service. Memories grow not in bulk only, but in significance with the years; the time comes when man's companionship is mainly with his own memories. It is a great matter therefore to Shibli Bagarag, a rich provision laid up in store for his age, that his mind is stored with noble memories; surely from the conning of them not boastfulness, but charity, mellower wisdom, will crown his after days. But while the delights of memory are permissible delights, Shibli Bagarag must not succumb to them. He would be but a dead man were he to wander among the tombs of the past reading its epitaphs on himself. Not as one wasteful of thought, brooding over the achievements of bye-gone days, but as one living in, finding the fruits of the past in the present, must the reformer seek his reward. It is in the betterment of the world, the glad consciousness that he has contributed towards its betterment, that his reward lies. In the words of the poet:

THE BALDNESS OF SHAGPAT

"The blush with which their
   folly they confess
Is the first prize of his supreme
   success."

A prize indeed this earthly, yet heavenly in its nature. Put it that no material
gains, that neither honours nor recognition of service were his, would it so
greatly matter when the world is given
unto him for reward? He has but to
witness its emancipation, its leap forward into light, to find recompense for
all his labours. Additional recompense
is his in that he is now secure of a
larger field and more commanding
opportunity for further labour. The
world never deposes, cannot indeed
depose its true leaders. Statesmen
hold office by the will of the people,
but reformers of the Shibli Bagarag
type by the will of God. Therefore he
is free to keep at the front of things,
not witnessing only but guiding the
world in its progress. It is a great
position and brings proportionately
great care, but where no care is neither
can there be joy. Man cannot afford
to part with his cares otherwise than
by triumphing over them; it is from

them that by the alchemy of spirit
he extracts all his purest, most abiding
joys. Precious indeed are Shibli Bagarag's spoils of victory; surely many
ambitious youths are nobly envious
of him, and of the kingship he has
achieved among men. But more precious by far than these is the music
of a voice speaking in the ear of the
reformer's soul, and 't is the voice of
the Divine One, the "well done good
and faithful servant" of the Master!

Thus far Shibli Bagarag. But we
also, to the extent that we have succeeded in interpreting the Allegory, are
entitled to look for spoils. It has
doubtless been good exercise for our
teeth, this cracking of Meredithian nuts;
but if the nuts have proved empty we
will consider we might have put our
teeth to better use. But they have not
proved empty. For myself I make
sorrowful confession in regard to some
of the daintiest and sweetest of these
Meredithian nuts that in my endeavour
to crack I have but clumsily crushed
them, sadly injuring the kernel. But
however I may have mangled the nuts,
even in the mangling I have proved

they are not empty, and that is some gain.

That my gains are not greater — viewing me no longer as nut-cracker — is not wholly my fault, for indeed they have been partly filched from me by magic. I always knew that fruit is never so sweet as when eaten fresh off the bush; and when I designed to fill my hamper from Meredith's Garden of Allegory, I reckoned on deterioration. Still I thought that as carried fruits go, I could give you some fair samples of the produce of the Garden. But alas, no sooner were the samples placed in my hamper than I noticed them, especially the best, the choice clusters of sap and beauty, undergo mysterious deterioration. No ordinary deterioration was it, but of a kind to vex and puzzle me, set me viciously chiding my own mishandling of the fruit. But now I know the secret. The land of Allegory is an enchanted land, and the law of its enchantment is that all fruits carried out of it suffer magical blight, some indeed being in a moment shrivelled into saplessness. Still if you inspect my hamper you may find some samples which have suffered less than others under this blight. I am not without hope that these samples may please you, maybe even induce you to visit the Garden for yourself, that you may pluck its fruit fresh from the bush.

My last word is no figure of speech, but a plain statement of a profound conviction. All that is best is for the young. A book which suits, nobly meets the noble needs of youth, is necessarily a great book. "The Shaving of Shagpat," written in his youth by a man who even to old age retained the heart of youth, is so pre-eminently a book of this quality that it will not have come by its own until it is taken as a *vade mecum* by the youth of the country. It is a gay teacher of profound wisdom. The truths it teaches are of such a nature that

> "Were men once clothed in
> them, we should create
> A race not following, but com-
> manding fate."

Trieste Publishing has a massive catalogue of classic book titles. Our aim is to provide readers with the highest quality reproductions of fiction and non-fiction literature that has stood the test of time. The many thousands of books in our collection have been sourced from libraries and private collections around the world.

The titles that Trieste Publishing has chosen to be part of the collection have been scanned to simulate the original. Our readers see the books the same way that their first readers did decades or a hundred or more years ago. Books from that period are often spoiled by imperfections that did not exist in the original. Imperfections could be in the form of blurred text, photographs, or missing pages. It is highly unlikely that this would occur with one of our books. Our extensive quality control ensures that the readers of Trieste Publishing's books will be delighted with their purchase. Our staff has thoroughly reviewed every page of all the books in the collection, repairing, or if necessary, rejecting titles that are not of the highest quality. This process ensures that the reader of one of Trieste Publishing's titles receives a volume that faithfully reproduces the original, and to the maximum degree possible, gives them the experience of owning the original work.

We pride ourselves on not only creating a pathway to an extensive reservoir of books of the finest quality, but also providing value to every one of our readers. Generally, Trieste books are purchased singly - on demand, however they may also be purchased in bulk. Readers interested in bulk purchases are invited to contact us directly to enquire about our tailored bulk rates. Email: customerservice@triestepublishing.com

You May Also Like

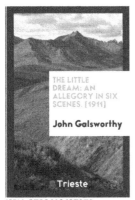

ISBN: 9780649637270
Paperback: 50 pages
Dimensions: 6.14 x 0.10 x 9.21 inches
Language: eng

The Little Dream: An Allegory in Six Scenes. [1911]

John Galsworthy

ISBN: 9780649692613
Paperback: 120 pages
Dimensions: 6.14 x 0.25 x 9.21 inches
Language: eng

Results of Astronomical Observations Made at the Sydney Observatory, New South Wales, in the Years 1877 and 1878

H. C. Russell

www.triestepublishing.com

You May Also Like

ISBN: 9780649587667
Paperback: 176 pages
Dimensions: 6.14 x 0.38 x 9.21 inches
Language: eng

Second Year Language Reader

Franklin T. Baker & George R. Carpenter & Katharine B. Owen

ISBN: 9780649738618
Paperback: 144 pages
Dimensions: 6.14 x 0.31 x 9.21 inches
Language: eng

Zoe: An Athenian Tale

J. C. Colquhoun

www.triestepublishing.com

You May Also Like

ISBN: 9780649420544
Paperback: 108 pages
Dimensions: 6.14 x 0.22 x 9.21 inches
Language: eng

1807-1907 The One Hundredth Anniversary of the incorporation of the Town of Arlington Massachusetts

Various

ISBN: 9780649194292
Paperback: 44 pages
Dimensions: 6.14 x 0.09 x 9.21 inches
Language: eng

Biennial report of the Board of State Harbor Commissioners, for the two fiscal years commencing July 1, 1890, and ending June 30, 1892

Various

You May Also Like

ISBN: 9780649199693
Paperback: 48 pages
Dimensions: 6.14 x 0.10 x 9.21 inches
Language: eng

Biennial report of the Board of State Harbor Commissioners for the two fisca years. Commeneing July 1, 1884, and Ending June 30, 1886

Various

ISBN: 9780649196395
Paperback: 44 pages
Dimensions: 6.14 x 0.09 x 9.21 inches
Language: eng

Biennial report of the Board of state commissioners, for the two fiscal years, commencing July 1, 1890, and ending June 30, 1892

Various

Find more of our titles on our website. We have a selection of thousands of titles that will interest you. Please visit

www.triestepublishing.com

Lightning Source UK Ltd.
Milton Keynes UK
UKOW01f1521231017
311488UK00008B/2260/P